Wisdom
and where to find it

BARRY LONG

BARRY LONG BOOKS

Barry Long Books are published by The Barry Long Foundation,
an educational charity registered in the United Kingdom.
Address: BCM Box 876, London WC1N 3XX.

First published for private circulation 1969.
Limited edition of the present text published 1994.
This new edition published 1996.

British Library Cataloguing-in-Publication Data:
a catalogue record for this book is available from The British Library.

Cover design: Rene Graphics, Brisbane, Australia.
Front cover photo: International Photographic Library.
Back cover photo: [Barry Long 1995]: Ambyr Johnston.
Typeset by Wordbase, London.
Printed in England on acid free paper by Alden Press, Oxford.

ISBN 1 899324 01 1

BARRY LONG, Australian writer and spiritual teacher, was born in 1926 and lives on the Gold Coast of Queensland. His uncompromising and practical approach to the truth of life attracts an increasing international audience.

WISDOM AND WHERE TO FIND IT contains transcripts of the five talks Barry Long gave when he first declared himself as a spiritual teacher in 1968. The book demonstrates the timeless starting point of his teaching and is a powerful introduction to self-discovery.

CONTENTS

The mystic death
1

The problem of choice
35

Why man must suffer
65

What man must do
89

Observation and meditation
105

Foreword

'WISDOM AND WHERE TO FIND IT', six simple words on a poster announced the invitation to come and listen to a man called Barry Long who would speak about truth, death and self-discovery.

On a November night in London in 1968, in a dingy Soho preview theatre, Barry Long gave the first of the five talks which are recorded in this book. Just fifteen people came, all earnest young men attracted by the spiritual quest for truth. No doubt each of them immediately sensed that they were in the presence of a remarkable man who is now widely regarded as one of the spiritual masters of the age.

Three years earlier to the day, on November 10th 1965, Barry Long had reached a critical point in the life-long process of his self-realisation and enlightenment – the point he called the 'immortal moment'. He had fled his native land of Australia and gone to India. He had abandoned his life as a family man and turned his back on a career as an ambitious journalist. For some time he had been inwardly questioning the values of the world around him and looking for more meaning and truth in life. Now, in the foothills of the Himalayas, his spiritual process put him through a period of isolation and emotional suffering as he faced the utter loneliness of being and having nothing. When the process was finished he had 'realised immortality' and passed through the mystic death.

Travelling on to England, he took work as a sub-editor on the London Evening News but this did not block the rapid process of his self-realisation. Whenever anyone at work would listen he spoke to them about the mechanical quality of life as it's normally lived, and the wonder of life when its truth is realised. These were thrilling words and one of his colleagues persuaded him to 'go public'. This young man arranged the series of talks in Soho, put up the posters and invited his own friends. Later he transcribed and edited the five talks and published them in a limited edition which circulated privately for many years before this present edition was published.

For young men and women of the 60's, stirred by social, political and creative revolution, this was a radical new voice; Australian, brash and unclouded by the intellectual politeness of the European intellectual. Barry Long offered a spiritual awakening uninfluenced by traditional religious paths; a matter-of-fact challenge to the considerate niceties of conventional spirituality. For him the life of truth was urgent, immediate, uncertain and ruled by a passion that confronted the false wherever it appeared. Those few people who came to the meetings in Wardour Street, Soho, were irreversibly impressed by the way Barry Long cut through their intellectual confusion and swept away the materialist conventions of so-called 'ordinary life'. They wanted more from him and quickly became his first students.

The Wardour Street Talks represent Barry Long's first declaration of himself as a spiritual teacher. Realisation is life-long and the expression of it as a teaching is constantly being refined. It was not until 1982 that his public teaching began in earnest. Since then he has spoken to very many audiences large and small around the world. Over the years his teaching has been honed with greater accuracy and his continuing enlightenment has penetrated to the core of what concerned him in the 1968 talks. Some of the terms and expressions used in this book have been superseded; yet it still contains a powerful teaching not otherwise in print.

The book addresses a mentality that in the spiritual seeker must necessarily be dispossessed of its illusions. For any individual to find the truth of life requires a conscious separation from mental structures and habits of thought. Barry Long challenges all beliefs and preconceptions and directs attention to a fundamental constant – the consciousness that lies at the centre of all our experience. In these talks (in his teaching at that time) he invites us to approach that consciousness through our understanding, a level of the mind absent of any memorable or conceptual knowledge.

The term 'understanding' connotes a degree of mental activity which Barry Long has utterly dispensed with in later teaching. His clarity of mind, stillness of consciousness and sheer presence of being now communicate much more directly. But men and woman are forever opening the same doors to self-discovery as those students did when they first encountered the truth of Barry Long in 1968. And while there is the need to understand or question life this book has a purpose. It is for all who would know the truth and the fact of life, who sense that somehow truth is not bound by the moral, ethical and intellectual concepts of what life is supposed to be about. And the talks remain a timeless testament to the central clarity that informs all of Barry Long's work. As you will read: 'Truth is forever. If you discover a truth now and years later bring your attention on to it again, you will find it still there, exactly the same, because truth never changes.'

The mystic death

THE REASON I PRESUME to speak to you of wisdom is that three years ago tonight I went through an experience which is called the mystic death. There are many deaths after it, but this is the first one in which wisdom as a totality can occur.

When we talk about wisdom, the wisdom of Solomon, the wisdom of men, we speak of a wisdom invariably related to objects outside ourselves. That, unfortunately, is not wisdom. That is an inferior wisdom, because the real wisdom, the wisdom that sleeps with you, worries with you, pines with you, weeps and laughs with you, is the wisdom of self-knowledge. This is the only wisdom.

I am going to talk for a short time and then invite you to ask questions. You may ask any questions concerning yourself. But what you will find yourself doing is going outside yourself, your own experience, because this is the momentum of the mind, where it gets its sense of power.

We are going to deal with the body, whose servers are the senses; the mind, whose food is knowledge; and one other thing which you are very rarely aware of, the very supporter of yourself — consciousness, whose food is understanding. It is your understanding I will be speaking to, not your knowledge. I do not care what famous philosophers you can quote, I am not interested in what they have said and nor are you tonight. What we are interested in is you. Because it is you who will die, it is you that is happy, it is you that weeps, it is

1

Who is being rhetorical, if I say "When Tony says on the one hand that understanding is "food" of conscious and o.t.oh. that he is speaking to our understanding tha

you that wishes, it is you that is frustrated. You, I speak to.

I am going to go over some ground so that we establish a cosmology or geography for us to wander through. If we don't do this and establish our terms we are not going to be able to travel the way of self-knowledge I am going to introduce you to.

The first rule of my teaching is, 'You must not believe me'. To believe anyone in the field of self-knowledge is not wisdom. You believe no-one, not even if he claims to be the greatest teacher on earth. It is not necessary. A thing is either true or not true in self-knowledge. You do not need anyone to tell you. An example is the question, 'Is it day or is it night?' Anything we talk about tonight will be as simple as that. To answer the question factually you will have to say 'It is night'. But if you are seduced by the mind out of self-experience and reply 'For the people in Australia it is day', you are going outside yourself. And this is what you will find the mind trying to do. To give the answer you have to imagine what the position is in Australia. That is the mind, trying to divide, trying to separate you from the moment — the cause of all worry.

But you must not believe me. What I say is either true or false or you do not understand.

The second rule of the teaching is, 'You must be true to yourself'. That means you must not allow your mind the comfort of doubt. This is the hardest rule. It demands tremendous humility, as you progress. For it means that if you think that what I say is not true, it is your duty to challenge me, and keep challenging me, until I satisfy your understanding. Otherwise you are wasting your time.

These rules are your protection. No faith is necessary. Nothing is necessary outside yourself. For an obvious reason. You have to assume that if self-knowledge is such a desirable thing, the aborigine alone and uncivilised in the centre of

Australia has the same facilities to know himself as the man who is able to read the philosophers. He has to have the same opportunity or there is no essential justice for man — and justice is then limited. Justice, we must assume, if the search is worth beginning, is unlimited — if only we can find it. It is certainly not found in the law courts. That is a type of justice that goes with the wisdom of things outside ourselves.

Only the individual can escape. The masses have no hope. The masses are eternally here, eternally bound, and eternally imprisoned. The individual, you, is the only one who can escape.

If almost everyone here walks out it does not matter. While there is one person to talk to it is worth my while to talk. This is because I am talking to you. This group has no hope at all. It will never be free, never realise itself. But you, the individual, can. The group clings together with ideas and knowledge outside itself.

What is this freedom we are looking for? What is this desire that all men feel sometimes in their lives when they are not going outside themselves and trying to possess things and knowledge? What is it that makes man say, 'Where am I going? What is it all about?' irrespective of how much he has achieved in the world? Why does he say this? Because he is seeking freedom — freedom from limitation, freedom from limitation of himself.

Each time you worry you limit yourself to that particular aspect of your life. If it is worry about your house, your bank account or your child, you immediately exclude the rest of your life which includes the beautiful park that you walk across, the grass that grows just as green as yesterday. You wipe all that out by an act of limitation and say 'This tiny relationship is my life'. For that time one concept fills your life. Now how could your life possibly be contained in one idea? By limitation, limitation imposed by the mind.

3

Frustration, disappointment, every worry is a limitation of yourself. What you are aiming at is to be free from this and it can be done only by freeing yourself of the habit of living outside yourself. This does not mean giving up things outside yourself. It is right that you must always do your duty and strive with the delight of striving — but you must match it with a corresponding self-knowledge. That will free you from limitation.

No-one can teach you truth. All I'm doing tonight is introducing you to yourself. Everyone has self-knowledge. Everyone of you has little pieces of it scattered around your consciousness, unrealised. All it needs is someone to bring them together, to link them up, so that they form a unity, a solid nucleus to go ahead with. The result will be that to-morrow, next week or next month, in the middle of your experience of life, you will suddenly say to yourself 'I see', and you will understand a truth. We have all done this. It is a moment of realisation.

When you leave here tonight you will have a greater mass, a new understanding of terms and yourself, a new way of looking at life as it really is — instead of seeing the limited view as you do now. I am going to push back your frontiers by pulling you together and making you more whole. To the degree you allow this to be done, the world will stand back from you and you can look at it with wisdom.

The trouble with worry is that we immerse ourselves in it, become identified, unable to stand back, and this leads to limitation. To limit your vision you must stand close. To delimit you must stand back.

In understanding wisdom there is a problem of memory. Knowledge can be remembered. Wisdom cannot. Wisdom or truth is discovered from moment to moment. If you ask anyone what wisdom or truth is you will get many unwise answers. Wisdom is the impartation of truth. In other words, the impartation of the fact to another person.

The hardest thing for man to see is the fact. It is because he cannot see the fact that he lives a life of almost continual disorder and limitation. He sees self-interest and mistakes it for the fact. He cannot distinguish between what is true and false. You will see examples of it tonight in your questions — I will have to keep pulling and pushing you back onto the fact. Because what you see will be something outside yourself.

To learn anything outside yourself — from arithmetic to how to drive a car — you absorb knowledge. You begin by saying 'I do not know'. Someone tells you ABC; you remember it and then it is yours — it becomes you. That is knowledge. But it is not understanding. Understanding lies behind knowledge. For instance, you could memorise the whole of the Bible without understanding it. Understanding is of consciousness, not of mind. The index of mind is reaction — yes and no; hot and cold; I agree, I don't agree; this is mine. All that is the world of mind. There are no answers there. Or we could say there are all the answers but no solutions. If you go around far enough the yes becomes no, the just becomes the unjust, the cruel becomes the merciful, the inquisition evolves from Christ's teachings. Round and round it goes. And it is you that is trapped in it, until you discover yourself. You are not of knowledge, you are of understanding.

Knowledge you can remember, because the mind lives off knowledge. Consciousness lives off understanding. You can remember knowledge but you cannot remember understanding.

When you leave this room tonight, when you go home and try to think of what I have said you are going to have trouble remembering. You will remember the parts that make a particular impact on your memory but you will not be able to remember all of it. If anyone asks you what I said you will soon find yourself faltering. You may pick up a particular point which you remember out of association and begin to elaborate on it, but the flow will die again. In this work you can give only as much as you understand.

Understanding is the very being of you. Understanding is the thing behind your smile that goes out to the child as you watch it play. It needs no words. When you love, when you are in the state of love, it is the same. When you hold hands with the one you love you do not think, do not remember, you just sit there. The tremendous thing about the state of love is that you can never experience it and think at the same time. But you must not believe me. You must look at it for yourself in yourself. This is where wisdom begins.

When you experienced love did you think? No. When you thought about doing something you lost the experience. But while you had it you sat there complete and content, requiring nothing, not even thought. When you think, love goes out the window. What is it that thrills in love, without thought, without the body moving. That's you, the real you. Your higher consciousness — above body, above mind.

You have the responsibility for a mind, which you act through, and your mind acts through a body, but each time you worry you come down off your throne, thrust yourself into your mind and into your body and look out from this cramped little body-world, limiting yourself to its immediate surround.

If you could stand back without thought you would be in the state of paradise while your body and mind enjoyed the state of awareness. It is not easy, it is very difficult. To hold it twenty-four hours a day is the hardest thing you will ever attempt.

You will notice that what I am talking about is the destruction of the creation as man knows it. If every man and woman on earth withdrew into consciousness, the world would run down. All men would be in paradise. But the world is not run like that. The world is run so that men who have realised the truth must come out of their paradise and do their duty while paradoxically still remaining there. Their duty, you will notice, is done in the world, where yours is. Their duty is to help free you. Your duty is to free yourself.

In consciousness there is no movement, no world. It is when consciousness comes into mind that the movement begins. Mind formulates the plans for the body to act in the world. Mind does not act in this world; it works through its instrument of body. In a moment I will show you how separate the worlds of mind and body are in your experience. It is the separation of these two in your understanding that we are after. Later you will separate from the mind. It all takes great pain and suffering and effort. Eventually you are in the world but not of it, eternally peaceful, eternally untouchable. This realisation is the mystic death.

I think I have covered enough ground now for us to know the direction we are going. Perhaps you would like to ask some questions?

You have been talking about you as an individual, a unit, or something that is one. Our experience is of many others. I don't quite understand how you would describe the relationship of the you to many you's.

This may not be easy to follow but the only thing that really exists for you is the 'you', the I who asked that question. Anything outside it is an object. It takes a tremendous bound of imagination for you to think I the speaker am an I too, in relation to you, because I am an object outside yourself.

What my teaching is concerned with is the I in you that asked that question. All these other people exist but they exist as a relationship. Everything exists as a relationship. But that I

7

in you who just spoke is the only relationship in the world where you can be sure of honesty, where there can be no mistake. This is because I can watch I, but you can never watch me the speaker because I might be lying and you will never really know. The one place you can be honest is in yourself, and that's where you have to be honest when I say you must challenge me.

Remember that I is not the mind; you only think it is because you have not separated. You are going to watch the mind, and the knower cannot be the known.

Mind is the enemy until it is known, mastered. Mind is the creator of division, always preventing unity. Wherever there is unity there is peace. Mind does not want peace — not while it is master, it only complains that it does. Mind lives off opposition and opposition is the opposite to peace.

Until a man separates he gets his I's mixed, so in the beginning he must get used to this primary idea of observing the I that appears to be him; — I am the thing that worries, I am the thing that is happy, I am the thing that pats the dog.

To me, the speaker, you are the thing that is worrying, but how do I know the feeling of worry that is in you? I can only imagine your worry from having worried myself. It is the same with a headache or any pain that moves us to sympathy. Through my self-knowledge of the pain and discomfort of having had a headache I can go out to you.

Every worthwhile response you will find is based on self-knowledge. It cannot be learned out of books; it is learned out of the pounding experience of life.

What do you understand by man and his duty?

You must do your duty from moment to moment. Your duty is what you have to do. Obviously, or why do you do it? This is a great mystery; it sounds crazy. It seems to make sense in a way — but something is missing. There does not appear to be a guide in it. But there is. The guide again is in I.

Let us have a look at it. Life is every moment. Life is not tomorrow evening, it is now. Every moment consists of its challenge. The totality of this and your response is your life, and somewhere in this lies your duty.

Man tends, whenever he gets a challenge, to react mechanically. It is something like when his body touches a hot stove and withdraws automatically. He acts on impulse from his mind, from the surface of himself, even though he may imagine he has thought about the problem. Man has to break this habit. He has to learn to live by referring every decision to himself, to his understanding. It is a beautiful way to live. It is a slowing-down, yet it results in a speeding-up of perception of knowledge and wisdom. It reduces the useless activity in us by eliminating our mechanical responses.

Every moment has a distinct duty for everyone. Man cannot do two things at the one time consciously. If he thinks he can, one of the actions is being done by his body, by habit. And habit is the opposite to conscious action. Man, the intelligent, begins with thinking and he cannot have two thoughts in his mind at the one time, either. By the same law he cannot have two duties at the same time. So, when he is in a state of indecision or conflict it means he has not slowed down enough to see his duty of the moment.

Where man goes wrong is that he is constantly dividing life into good and bad. He begins with his own self-interest, then his family's, then his country's, then humanity's and then the world's. Any time he has between he spends on dividing what happens to his neighbours and friends and anyone he hears about into good and bad. This keeps him frantically busy and unable to distinguish what really concerns him.

There is no rigid good and bad as the mind would have us think. They are created by a limited point of reference, by limited self-interest. It is here that ignorance and limitation begins.

How often do we take the course that is against our duty because it suits our self-interest? What is self-interest? It is good if I gain and bad if I lose. It is as simple as that. Gain and loss here apply to knowledge, money, people, experience — everything. If someone dies what do I lose? I lose the sight of them, the reassuring sense-knowledge that they exist. I lose a centre of production of knowledge for me. Because the mind strives to possess everything it desires, the greater the sense of exclusive possession, the greater the sense of loss. I am unhappy because I have lost a source of knowledge. This is a difficult fact to realise. We will leave it for another time. Man is happy when he gains, unhappy when he loses . . . but life is not run like that.

Life is run like this . . . all things that are, are good. It takes great wisdom to see it. You will not see it in its entirety tonight. But you will see it and live it one day — if you come this way.

I wouldn't say they were all good. I'd say they were all necessary.

Anything that is necessary is good, or it cannot be.

I hope you understand that I use the questions to go around the whole teaching. I seldom answer yes or no.

I am still not clear on duty.

I was saying man can have only one duty at a time. Sometimes man's duty or function is to fail. He would never select that one. He'll select the one, if he can, that will succeed. And it is right that he does. Man should never select failure, but failure occurs. His duty is to do his duty to the best of his ability. The result, though, is not for the individual alone. It is for life. So man must sometimes fail. But isn't his sense of failure, like his sense of bad, another limitation? Another assertion of self-interest? Isn't his sense of failure a denial of necessity, the total good?

From now on when you are faced with a decision you will ask yourself 'What is my duty?' You will refer it to your inner-self. You do this already, but not as a self-conscious act. In the beginning there will seem to be no precise answer. You must do your best and persevere, for this thing inside you is your own higher-consciousness. It does not reveal itself easily. Like all things worth having it takes great effort. Even though you do not realise it, it will be guiding you.

Remember, what you attempt may still fail from the limited point of view but you will have the tremendous satisfaction of knowing that you did your duty by trying to go inside. You can do no more. Eventually certainty will come and you will know this way of living is the only way for you. Do not be discouraged. Remember it is practised in the midst of life. You might be late for work and have promised to collect your sister's dress from the cleaners. She needs it desperately, but if you stop off for it you will be late. Which is your duty, the work or the dress? There is only one place to find out . . . and remember, the time is in the moment. Man seldom does this. He looks at the surface of himself, at what he can get away with to suit his passing mood. And, of course, at the same level he finds his excuses.

You say this learning is a minority thing? Why? Why can't it be a majority thing?

If truth were available to the majority the creation would not continue as it is. All would be peace and happiness, the states that man imagines he aims for. That is not the object of

11

the creation, or it would exist now. The object as far as you are concerned is to free yourself of the creation. When you are free you will be able to answer the question for yourself by trying to give wisdom to the masses and see what they do to you.

What about helping the poor and afflicted?

Man cannot free the poor. If he goes and works for the spastic children it is good, but let him not delude himself that he is helping them. He is helping their bodies, but man is not the body. The only way you can ever help man is by discovering freedom for yourself and then helping him towards his freedom. Man has to be made non-dependent on anything, otherwise how can he ever be free? You cannot call yourself free if you are dependent on a government, or if you are dependent on a human body. The body might be maimed and perhaps killed tomorrow and that would be the end of you.

The truth is man has no end and is dependent on nothing, not even life, if he probes deep enough within himself. You must do that.

Something within man tells man he is immortal. If not, why are you not scared to death now . . . because you are going to die, whether in fifty years or tomorrow. What is it that stops man from seeing this? He knows — though his mind does not — that he is immortal. Not the body though, and not the mind. The mind is not immortal, the mind is mortal, and the mind consists of all your opinions. Every opinion you hold has got to go, because opinions are not true. Your understanding is true — it will go on — it is immortal. But what is your understanding? All the masters who gave us the great religions knew, but most of the wisdom died with them. After a master's death his teaching is corrupted by minds.

All the masters have required their students to make certain sacrifices, such as giving away their possessions or turning the other cheek. They know the only way to truth is for man to become less. They know it is man's opinions or impressions that he is secure or that he has been wronged that make him feel bigger. These sacrifices are aimed purely at breaking habit, the mechanical in you.

If you observe yourself in action you will see you consist almost entirely of habit. Each time you have an argument you trot out the same argument for that occasion or until you find a better one. In discussion you produce over and over the points picked up from others and give them out as your own, but you cannot come up with any permanent arguments. This is because you are changing — this is the world of mind, the world of opinions and impressions.

You cannot be free while you hold the opinion a man has wronged you. Until you can say with understanding, 'No man can wrong me. I have an essential dignity that can never be touched', and live it — you are in the world. The thing that will guide you to your duty will also protect your essential dignity.

A strange thing, this. The great masters have exhorted men to turn the other cheek because they know the only way man can experience his own real and unshifting beauty and dignity — the fact of it, not the opinion of it — is by destroying or denying his self-assertion. Once this has been discovered let any man try to step upon the dignity of such a man — the whole world would crash upon him. But this, of course, is a long way through the deep crust of opinion that encircles us.

It is the dying to opinions and impressions, the dying to the habit of reaction, that is so painful on this way to wisdom.

Why doesn't man listen to the teachers?

He can't listen. He has too many opinions to listen. The hardest thing for a man to do it to listen. If half the people here tonight are listening I would be very surprised. Listening is an act of humility. You have to just sit there and deny the assertion of your own opinions. What usually happens is we listen on one side and keep our opinions intact on the other; that is not enough in this teaching. You are not allowed to keep your opinions. You have to stand up and spit them out at me and quote your philosophers if you have to — have them answered, dissolved, by your own understanding. But the mind is not as honest as that. It holds back with its opinions, resurrects them when the destructive light of truth is removed and it feels secure again in its own world of ignorance and self-assertion. For you, the seeker, this is doubt.

If you are sincere, do not worry; this thing will not let you go. But within the week you are likely to find the mind trying to divide you from the teaching. As I said, you may start to doubt: you may see the man and the not the message.

Doubt is a form of cowardice if you have found a source of truth. You have to become the master of your mind. You have to have the guts to say 'All right Mind, you are trying to separate me from something that a week ago thrilled or delighted me. One of us was wrong. I insist that we go to the source and you have your say there'. If you cannot come you can always telephone or write a letter. You will find you were right, for your mind cannot ask any question in self-knowledge that my understanding cannot answer. But the mind would rather slink away and mumble 'He is a phoney'. Why? Because the mind is the most potent instrument in the creation, and the creation's duty is to create, not simplify.

If the mind or the creation can force you away from self-knowledge it will. Everything in the world is designed to keep you away from it . . . your children, your bank account, your food, everything. They are there to keep you immersed, so that when the opportunity comes to turn within you are too busy burying your father.

Why aren't there more people here tonight? How many scores of thousands read the advertisements offering 'Wisdom and where to find it?' No-one wants wisdom because no-one believes living man can speak wisdom. Why? Because we all have our own opinions of what wisdom is. Man as mind cannot speak to man of wisdom. The man has to disappear, die, and make way for the message. Then he is a teacher. The mind in absence remembers the man. Do not let it fool you.

Isn't there a great unfairness in that the majority are on the steps of enlightenment but nobody comes along to assist them?

It is true that the progression of life of all things is towards enlightenment, but it is an eternity in time. It is also true that all men to exist have to have self-knowledge. To become a man, which is individual consciousness, the entity has to have a specific degree of self-knowledge. That is the leaping point.

Justice is complete and perfect, and those who are ready always get a teacher. It is impossible for anyone who is ready not to be provided with a teacher.

Here, I am going to introduce an aspect that may be premature. Man is not just one life. Man has many lives. But people make the mistake of thinking the mind lives again, the little personality they cherish as themselves. It does not. Mind and its knowledge dies. It is his understanding which recurs. That is not the man as we know him now, unless he lives and speaks only truth. Then it is still not himself, because no man exists really. Only his understanding goes on. His opinions and the rest of him dissolve over a period of say, a million recurrences — we will try not to use rebirth. It is a wrong word. To use words like rebirth and reincarnation we have to use a mind image which suggests some sort of personal

15

survival. It is false. In the same way we talk of life after death, but life after death is not life after death, it is a continuation of the stupidity and limitation of our current life. That is no good. We don't want that or you would not be here tonight.

When you die nothing changes. You go on with the same limited visions, only the cosmology and its laws are wider and its substance finer and more intense. But you go on, creating by your habit the same world around you. You are no closer to God than you are now. No closer to wisdom or truth, although unconsciously you are because of the tremendous impact of death upon the being. Death in itself is a total traumatic experience, a massive shock, a realisation of beauty, fulfilment and promise. And death is all that life is — a continuous traumatic experience that produces understanding.

Returning to the question, when a man is ready he gets a teacher. Many get a teacher and still don't hear. It is not the object to free the masses, so the masses do not need a teacher. As soon as a teaching reaches the mass level it will be corrupted and not understood. Is there any teaching less understood than Christianity? Or Hinduism, Shintoism or any other which the masters formulated? They are not only misunderstood, they are not even read.

I am not convinced of something. If you play a game you must be able to lose. You said the whole universe is progressing towards God, enlightenment, totality, whatever you term it. Yet I feel you must be able to lose the game and fail. Call it hell or whatever you like — kaput, finish, out of the race. Am I wrong in this?

Yes. Because there is no race.

But it is a race in a way, isn't it?

16

Man does lose the race, in a sense — each time he turns his back on a source of truth he has found. When he dies and goes to what he calls his heaven he is not content with heaven. Heaven becomes hell for man. He chooses then to return to earth.

You could say he then loses the race, because the thing that returns is not him — he can never remember who he was. In that context he loses the race, but he does not really, because it is all part of the great movement.

What is heaven?

It is quite easy to discover what heaven will be for most men. It would be a place where everything he desired came true. This is obviously what he is striving to create here. Our heaven will be what we are looking for here. It is a place where every wish comes true — except the wish for wisdom. You won't get that there, unless you have desired and striven for it here.

From what you say heaven is a place of final satisfaction.

Of mind.

No. It is the ultimate. It is beyond all the lives you ever lead. And you must have passed through heaven in your journey or you would not recognise it when you come to it. It cannot be unknown to you.

While you are journeying you will never find heaven. You don't journey to heaven. Heaven is now.

That is the basis of my argument. Heaven is not something we are promised. We will come to it.

17

I did not say you were promised. You have gone outside your own experience.

This is where it is difficult. To get your answer you have to ask yourself this question: What is heaven to me now? What would I think of heaven as now? Because you are the enjoyer now, you are the I now, there is nothing else outside you to experience heaven. Heaven is now. So what delights you now will be your heaven now.

You can never go outside of now. Now, what would delight you twenty-four hours a day — somewhere, twenty-four hours a day in the same state. No, that heaven is not for you. That heaven is not for any man — unless he can walk in the world twenty-four hours a day and still be in heaven. That is man's heaven, now — but not the next man's, now. Your heaven might be a place where you can sit quietly in yourself in being or in meditation, three hours a day. That's a much higher heaven — if we can use the word higher and we can as I will illustrate — than the heaven of a man who cannot sit quietly for thirty seconds, a man who has got what the world calls an active mind and admires, who boasts he needs continual stimulus. This person's heaven won't be the other man's. And you'll notice now why we can say a person's heaven is higher than the other. The person who relies on stimulus is depending on something outside himself. To the degree he does this his heaven will be lower, because if he ever goes to a place where there is no thing he will be unable to exist. That place is the highest heaven — self-sufficiency, where there is nothing that can be removed.

The busy man's heaven will be busy and complicated. The other man's will be unbelievably simple, dependent on one fact alone — I am. Put the first man suddenly into that heaven and he would disintegrate, become a raving lunatic, his mind destroyed by the aloneness of it. That is the great justice; why God, or whatever it is, keeps him recurring. In every life he eliminates some more desire roots. This gradually reduces his dependence on things outside himself and raises him to higher and higher heavens.

How are his desires eliminated?

Desire works like this. You desire food. You eat. Where is the desire? It no longer exists. A desire filled is freedom from the stress of its wanting.

The body is one big continuous desire. Therefore the experience of hunger recurs. So is the desire for power the recurring catalyst in man.

Say a man wants to be the boss. This is part of the desire for power. He strives for years and becomes the boss, having sacrificed many other desires to get there. If he is ready for a realisation he will look around him and say 'Good God, after all that I'm still not free'. Or, 'What I thought I was striving for is not here at all'. If he realises this sincerely, an aspect of the desire for power is filled, ended for him — a chink of freedom from rebirth.

It is his unsatisfied desires that keep man recurring. Without desires he would be in heaven twenty-four hours a day, walk through the world untouched. In his heaven man gets all his desires granted except one — the desire for power.

If everyone's desire for power is filled what is the point of it? There is no-one to have power over. Satisfaction of the desire for power is in overcoming something. Its ultimate is in overcoming other men. You can overcome by building a dam — but that is the beautiful in man, when he performs as an instrument of life. But he is not satisfied with that; he strives for power for power's sake.

I don't agree with you. I don't agree that everybody wants power. You say creating something does not satisfy you — I

agree with that because you want to create something better.
You want power over yourself but not over another man.

That is a very good question. You must look at it very closely. Man is made up of four desires — the desires for position, prestige, possessions and permanence. They all add up, if you look at it closely enough, to the desire for power.

You might think of power as controlling someone, when you can tell them what to do without the fear of their disobeying you. But power is a much more subtle thing. Even to exist is a desire for power, a self-affirmation that is impossible without power over something inferior to yourself. You must have food, you must cut down the tree, you must destroy many things to exist, and this is a right power-desire for the body. But the body's desires are not our problem, our problem is in the desires of the mind which lives off the power of knowledge. An example is when we are offended because someone is not courteous to us. Why do we desire others to be courteous? Because courtesy is the oil that allows our selfish, power-driven egos to live together. If I smile and thank you, everything is all right. I tacitly recognise your existence, reaffirm the self-assertion of your action. If I don't, I insult you because I take from you by failing to acknowledge the power of being you felt as that action.

Man, as power, does not like to be taken from. He never wants to be the breeze, or the rain, or the apple, or the sheep that serves without looking for self-aggrandisement. That is why the man said 'Turn the other cheek'. A man who can do that is denying the desire for power — denying himself.

The desire for power is unbelievably subtle. Our desire to be identified with famous people, even if they are notorious, is an example. As long as the person is not a murderer, which is likely to make people recoil and ignore our existence by avoiding us, we don't mind being mentioned as an acquaintance of the man. In other words, if our association with a person attracts the prestige of favourable attention to us, we are happy. Who can resist name dropping? Why do we do it? We want others to look up to us, envy us. And we experience the subtle, stroking warmth of power like the workman who touches his cap to the boss. We've all done it. We've all said 'Good morning, Mr Smith' — and walked past the office boy. This is the desire for power — to associate ourselves with the greater.

In his heaven man cannot get this power. No-one wants to be the slave — unless they are servile by nature; and you will find them in heaven too. They get their delight out of being servile. But servility is not humility; servility is a form of self affirmation. The servile ego is just as big as the next one, because it lives on servility and not surrender. The power you have to aim for, the power that is not corrupting, that you have to win here on this earth, is the power over yourself.

Man's life is desire power. Everything he does is based on desire power. Man thinks he has will power; he is mistaken. Man does not have will power — he has desire power.

But to live in this world we have to use the nastiness. You don't want to, but to get on you have to. Yet the other side of you pulls you back and says 'Don't do it'. You go for a few days happily not doing it then you say 'I've got to do it, I have got to join them'.

Otherwise you'll go under, won't you?

Yes.

This is man's greatest conflict. This is the problem of the good man. I'd like to get every good man and strip him open and see how much is good of him. It is impossible to be a

21

good man and be honest with yourself. There are no good men. There are good-acting men, but there are no good men.

Goodness lies inside the man, even unexpressed. There is badness in all men. But it is the way of things that we are allowed to have good men who are able to conceal their badness while other men cannot.

We need good men or the whole thing would fall into absolute chaos. But a good man is never a wise man. Wisdom begins with good men and crushes and smashes them.

There is only what is — the fact. And goodness is not a fact, because it needs badness to exist. Anything that cannot stand alone is not a fact; it is a concept, an impression. So goodness, unfortunately, is false, and so is badness. When you have this realisation you have entered the world of wisdom — but you cannot have it unless you have been a good person.

A good person is someone who does not desire to intrude upon his fellow men. He has intruded, definitely has, and has seen himself do it much to his own shame, but he has also begun to see — as you have — that he has to get in there and do these things.

A good person begins and ends there. Now comes wisdom. His goodness has got to be taken from him as well as his badness. And it is the destruction of these concepts in him that rips a man open on this way, puts him into a state of absolute confusion. Yet, while this is happening, the essential guide within him protects him by insisting 'What is your duty, my son? You must always do your duty'.

That is why you must develop this practice of looking inside. As you destroy goodness and badness as concepts you have to have infallible help and that is only to be found within you. This, of course, is a very advanced stage in man's development and is impossible for the majority to grasp.

All men want to be good, but you can't be good. You've got to get in there and join them.

You do your badness with your body; if you talk about a man behind his back it is your body that talks. Your mind is the manipulator but your body has got to do it. What you have got to do is separate from it, like a real man, and say to yourself, 'Shut up'! You have to die a little. Deny yourself. But man can't shut up. How many times have we known something about someone and said to ourselves 'I will not say it'; and yet heard ourselves say it. It is so depressing. But eventually you realise you have to do certain things in this world, just as you have to succeed and fail. So you have to be good and bad, but only in the moment.

If you believe right is beyond goodness and badness and work towards your aim you may do what society considers to be wrong. It is like the thing that carries explorers and tyrants on — be that right or wrong they go beyond society's concepts.

That is so. They are instruments. The infallible guide for you against self-indulgence in choosing your duty is the question, 'Am I prepared to pay the price without complaint or excuse if I fail?' The answer of a sincere person has to be 'Yes, even if they kill me and take everything, even my honour'. This is the attitude of a courageous man or woman. Most of us, when we have a choice and choose with self-interest, will try to lie our way out of the consequences or make excuses. The man or woman who knows where he or she is going and acts on duty says 'I do not care what they say. It is right for me'. And this is just what tyrants do. But they do not do it in the right way, the conscious way. They do it as instruments. Our way is to do all things consciously, so that we eventually separate from the instrument and become something else, conscious, above it.

If you look closely at your life you will see you are an instrument of life. You are going in a certain direction. Not

23

the way you plan because all the instruments of life go round in a circle. The mind tries to go in a straight line — your way. The mind says 'It is good — I must be honest'. It then discovers halfway along the way to honesty that it can't be honest because there is no such thing as honesty. Honesty can only go so far. Then you have to live in the world, as you have found, and be dishonest. What do you do then? The person seeking wisdom says 'Well, if I must be dishonest, I will be dishonest consciously and if I am caught I will make no excuses — I will not compromise'.

You will notice the word 'consciously'. All this is a matter of becoming conscious — to do everything in your life consciously. We live twenty-three-and-a-half hours a day doing this unconsciously. You have to develop the habit of being conscious by breaking the habit of being unconscious. It is the hardest thing a man can do. The way is to observe yourself — the way you walk, and so on. I will go into this in a later talk.

Self-observation is extremely difficult because we continually identify with our environment which is our relationships. And we cannot separate: worry follows because we are identified with a limited view of ourselves. Many of the tyrants have said 'I do what I do without any excuses' because they are very big men playing for very big stakes. The same attitude has to be lived by the little man. He is a tyrant himself with power over many relationships. For what else is his sense of personal choice? But he has to be prepared to be shot for it — like the tyrant — by dying in a million little ways, consciously.

So this is your test: when you have to decide your duty be sure you go the rest of the way — be prepared to pay the price. This is your protection against your cunning self, the mind. It will do anything to choose the comfortable way and lie and justify itself out of a situation. Eventually, you will realise there are no reasons, justifications or excuses for anything. There is only the fact. This is another dying you have to experience on the way to wisdom.

I was speaking to you earlier about the mystic death. The mystic death is the first death, a psychological death, in which man experiences immortality. The process is mechanical; everything is mechanical. Even heaven is mechanical. But you can only see this when you are above it. All things are done by laws; the mystic death is no exception. It occurs at a point where the person has died to most of his or her desires. It is preceded by great pain and agony as you would imagine, because most of the desires for power, position, prestige, possessions and permanence have to go.

This includes the desire to express your opinion, desire for money, for security, desire to worry — just about everything that man consists of. Take from any man his house, his bank account, all he possesses, his loved ones, then take his ideas of honesty and dishonesty, his opinions of what is right and wrong — and what has he got left?

When you reach that stage you die — while still in the body. You pass straight through death. The pain is so terrible there is nowhere to go but out.

It is not an escapist death, just the opposite. You have to stand there, unflinching, as death sweeps over you. And you burst through. You see what immortality is. All you have done, you realise, is shed what is false in man. You realise that all those desires I have mentioned depend on things outside yourself.

Man's opinions represent his dependence on knowledge. In this death you are not allowed to retain your knowledge as such because it is a clinging, a self-security. It has to go.

It cannot be done by renunciation, by saying 'I give up all my money'. You give up nothing doing that. If you have money then what is is best. Enjoy it, do what you like with it. It's only your body that will use it. You can get drunk every

25

day or buy a thousand motor cars. There is nothing wrong with having possessions, but there is something in the possessor that has to be removed. And that is what this death is — the removal of the self-interest, the clinging.

It is man's clinging that makes him put a fence around his backyard. If his clinging is removed his attitude is: 'Everything is mine. Why do I need to put a fence up. The blue sky is mine what can you take from me?' But the action of mind is to divide, to separate, to say 'This is mine'. So he puts a thing automatically inside a mental fence.

I'm not talking about putting up a fence for security — this is necessary in a different world. I'm talking about mental fences, attitudes. Mind's attitude is always, 'This is mine, to have and to hold. You just try to step on my opinions and see what you get'. This is the fenced-off property that we consist of. That's why the man exhorted us to turn the other cheek. He knew we had to break these habits of what we expect, what is right, what is wrong. There is only the fact that all things are right, to be. That you can do nothing of yourself except in yourself, by right attitude, by doing your duty.

What do you do if another tries to stop you in your duty? Having satisfied yourself that it is a right aim, you persevere, using your intellect through your own understanding of what is right and what wrong. But man tries to take his right and wrong from the ten commandments or some other rigid concept. He cannot do that. He cannot take his right and wrong out of a book, out of what some philosopher has laid down. He has to go into himself, into his essential being, and say 'What is right and wrong for me?'

As you yourself have seen, what is right and wrong for each of us differs. And yet, by the great essential unity and, dignity of life, what is right for men who live this way is somehow right for all. Perhaps it will mean pain for others, and yourself, but remember, man progresses on pain.

The only reason you are here tonight is because you have suffered pain. When man asks the question 'What is life all about?' it is because he has felt frustration and limitation, which is pain. Pain is the only way to freedom, but it does not last forever because sorrow exists only while you exist, while you are losing yourself. And that is all death is.

The dropping of the body is not death — you are not the body. I will give you an illustration. Say I have a child; someone runs in and says 'Your child has been killed by a car'. I am shocked. I weep — a natural reaction. I experience all the dreadful feelings of loss. Then I am informed it is all a mistake, my child is alive and well. Now I am happy. What happened in fact? Nothing. What was the thing in me affected? Not the body but something else. Something that apprehended loss. That is the entity that we depend upon in our daily life. See how easily misled it is. What misled it? Knowledge, false knowledge.

Self-knowledge is never false, never deluding, because you always know whether you are doing the right or wrong for you. It keeps nudging you if you are doing wrong, but man keeps pushing it away. Finally he becomes so used to doing this he can live with it, as he can live with a headache. But if you are true to yourself, referring everything within every day, every hour, you will find that if it is wrong for you, you cannot act. Conversely, you may find you have to act even if it ends in disaster for you.

How often have we all known we were going to do something wrong and still done it? Could it be that wrong we did was right? That the wrong we apprehended was only the feeling that we would probably have to suffer. As he is, man is an instrument. The only way he can rise above this duality is by separation and continuous reference within, until he becomes the thing within.

We tell our children it is right to act in a certain way all the

27

time. It is a lie, but it sounds good. This is acting out of mind, out of memory, out of someone else's book. That cannot dictate what is right for you. It can help while your understanding is limited but even the child soon wakes up to what is happening. But instead of shouting 'It's all lies' he keeps quiet because it serves his self-interest — and he goes to sleep for the rest of his life like we all did before him.

Remember, all I am doing tonight is re-affirming what you have already experienced within yourself. Now you have heard it expressed, now you know it was not a random experience but a part of the sum of self-knowledge that is your deeper self. You will hear yourself saying 'I've been doing this for a long time. This is simple'. Of course it is simple. The whole process is simple. Truth is simple. The light is on or it is off. We are the complication.

I want to stop wanting . . .

By wanting . . . that is how you end wanting, and then watching what wanting is, and discovering what its essence is. By observing what wanting is you understand wanting. And after you have observed yourself — how you want, what you want, why you want, and who wants — you understand it.

If you want to understand a child at play you have to watch it, unobserved and silent. So you have to understand wanting. That is why man has to go through so many experiences in his life.

Perhaps I am going beyond the scope of this talk, but I will say it: man has to have been the murderer and the murdered, the thief and the victim, the accuser and the accused. For only by the experience can his understanding become total enough for him ever to leave the world.

So only by wanting can man ever be freed of wanting. But his trouble is he becomes identified with his wanting so that he cannot observe it. He is the wanting. Just as when I am angry I am anger. There is no me when I am angry. I am anger. My kindness, my compassion, my bank account, all vanish. The only way I can understand anger, to be free of it, is to step back and watch what is angry. As soon as I do, anger starts to disappear, because it is false. And so is wanting false, but it has to be watched, to be seen, and it takes a real man or a real woman to do it. In the midst of your raging desire you have to separate and watch it seething. It might take years, but eventually it will start to wilt. It doesn't like to be watched and it starts to fall away. The wanting becomes less urgent, so does the disappointment and the frustration: and the success, except that the delights of real success come, the success of having understood yourself. So that you never want what you do not want, and eventually you give up wanting.

Does this mean you won't exist? No, you'll still have your wants, but what you want you'll get, because you are then in tune with the harmony of life.

Why should a man want choice? Why should he have to choose? I tell you, you don't have to want anything — it will all be done for you by the great movement of life. You will never fail. You will only want when it is worthwhile. This state is achieved by watching wanting.

It cannot be false then. If anything, it is a step.

Yes, it is a step. But every step is false because it is below, and it falls away. You don't need it again. Then you look back and say 'Oh, I see the secret of life. Everything that is is right for me to use as a step until I get above it. Then I look down and see it is still right for all who follow, but it is now false for me'. Everything in your life is there as a step towards freedom. This is a tremendous truth, this having to pass through a thing to be free of it.

The whole progress and process of self-knowledge is the discovery of what is false. Everyone quotes the Greek philosopher who said 'Man, know thyself'. But no-one, including the philosopher, tells you how. Typically they repeat the words of truth without wisdom. I will tell you how. It will all be done by you, not by me. My job is to awaken your understanding. Yours is to make the effort. It is a long process.

The strange thing is that you never find out who you are. Of course, when you go through the mystic death and experience immortality you must realise it in relation to yourself, but you never find that self. The more you keep going within, you find wisdom, power, peace, paradise, God, but you won't find yourself. All you will ever discover is what is false, the step below you, for there is no end.

The key to self-knowledge is the practice of self-observation. So let us have a look at some of the things man is composed of.

Take anger: Say man begins work on himself; for a start he decides to observe himself being angry. Now, there is a law of life that helps us here. If you observe anything in yourself that is false it will begin to drop away. There is no exception to this law. What is false cannot stand the gaze of consciousness, and you will find you cannot observe yourself and be angry. You have to be identified to be angry.

Next; let us say you decide to observe the lies you tell. Man is an habitual liar; he lies for no reason at all. Who hasn't observed themselves telling a deliberate lie for no apparent reason? Most of our lying is mechanical. Once you begin observing your lying you separate from it and you start lying less. Man can never abolish all his lying; not while he is man — because man is a lie. He is made up of anger, greed, envy and various false states, which in their individual aggregate are a living lie; he might get rid of anger but he will never get rid of lying.

One of the last things to go is wanting, desire. And what is man but desire? He desires to breathe, eat, talk. Put him alone for a while and his personality starts to drop away. Why? Because mind desires stimulus to keep it active. Without stimulus it begins to go quiet and cannot support the falsehood of its personality.

Can't it be the other way as well?

If you mean looking, yes. Looking inward is the same in its effect as being in a dark cell. Put a person in a dark cell without any human contact and his personality will start to drop away. He will either go mad or start talking to himself in a mechanical attempt to create an alternative stimulus. This produces a pathetic inbred half-personality.

If a man goes within himself while acting in the world it is the same as being in the cell — only this way he consciously destroys his false personality by observation and discovers his essential self, its dignity, its personality and reality. But the other man whose personality drops away has nothing left except fear and insecurity. What he is, is the product of his 'looking out'.

Is there a residue of all these falsehoods that one retains in terms of understanding in the essential self?

Oh yes.

This is the relationship between the mind and understanding?

Yes. Mind is the thing between. There is life which is experience.

That gives sufficiency?

31

Yes. Living is the fire. In chemistry if we want a change we put the substance in the fire in intense heat and that gives us the action. The individual life or living is the fire; the mind comes next, and at the top of it is intellect which allows us to formulate the results through reason.

Reason is the faculty that allows us to line up the facts of our experience in a logical and coherent fashion. If I give you the words 'chair, dog, grass' reason cannot get going because reason's function is to line-up facts towards a conclusion. If I say 'room, light, leisure, people' reason can begin to work. Mind is there to correlate the experience with its knowledge, resulting in the understanding of pain, unhappiness or indifference. In that way we understand the effect of a headache. In other words, the experience passes through the mind into understanding as pain while the knowledge goes into memory.

You can get a glimpse of justice in connection with recurrence here. You will remember I said understanding is the recurring factor in man and that his knowledge dissolves on rebirth. How could recurrence work justly if knowledge were the recurring factor? The man born in 1066 would have nowhere near the same potential knowledge as the man born in the seventeenth century. But the potential for understanding was the same in 1066 as in 1968 because the effects of relationship are virtually infinite. Consequently the I of relationship remains the same.

But no doubt there is a slight overall shift in that the potential for experience becomes greater as the world's knowledge becomes greater — knowledge being only greater multiplicity. So what you said was right. Life, the experience, the fire, is apprehended by mind as memory and by consciousness as understanding.

As you continue to know yourself you will end up with consciousness. It is the experience of consciousness that is immortality, for it is consciousness that you carry forever with you through all your rebirths. But going the other way, when your body drops away, you carry with you your mind. Your consciousness is unrealised unless you have realised while in the body. So nothing changes, and in heaven you will fill all your desires, or seem to.

The great truth is that desire has to be filled on the earth. It has to have the original matter which is the origin of desire. For desire is a primal, earthly thing. Man's desire-heaven is an ethereal place. The closer you get to the ethereal or, ideally, non-form, the closer you are to understanding.

Understanding is the disappearance of desire. So desire has to be filled in the grossness of the world from where it emanates. We cannot imagine the heaven that is all under-standing. We can however experience it in meditation as a state requiring nothing. End of desire. End of all worlds.

Couldn't you argue that this is nothingness, that all men will die and become nothingness and achieve nothingness?

Yes, you could do that if you wanted to. But that would be a denial of yourself. Could you try to argue now against the tremendous reality of self-existence?

The problem of choice

I WILL RUN OVER QUICKLY what we spoke about last week. I told you there was only one place to find wisdom and that was in yourself. It is not found in books and it is not found in opinions. It is found in you; and the only limitations to wisdom in you are the limitations you place upon yourself. Opinions are man's main limitation. Until he goes beyond opinions into what is true or false, and especially into the humility of knowing he does not know, he cannot be free. To not know demands the attitude of listening. You cannot listen if you have an opinion; you only think you can.

I gave you the first two rules of this teaching. The first was: you should not believe me. In wisdom it is not wise to believe anyone. The attitude of mind is: I don't know but I will find out — and the action is to continuously look for the answer within yourself, that is, within your own experience. The example I gave of this was the question — is it day or night? You have to reply it is night. Truth is as simple as that; the difficulty is the seeing it. What stands between truth and us is our opinions. So, the first rule is that you must not believe me.

The second rule is: you must be true to yourself. That means, if you feel I am misleading you, misrepresenting the fact, you must challenge me and keep challenging me. You have to refuse your mind the satisfaction and comfort of doubt.

I said we talk about three things in this teaching. The first is the body, whose feeders are the senses. The second is mind whose food is knowledge. The third is consciousness whose food is understanding. If I speak to your knowledge we will have an argument. Knowledge always has an opposite and to preserve its own existence it insists that all men are entitled to their opinion. In wisdom, all men are not entitled to their opinion. A thing is either true or it is false.

Tonight's talk was to have been 'Why man must suffer'. It seems to me that it has been changed to 'The problem of choice'. As I get on to choice you will understand why I have had to change it. I never know for certain what my subject will be — because I do not have a choice; just as in the highest realisation man discovers that his freedom is contained in choicelessness. A strange truth this, because it would seem that choicelessness is the denial of life itself. And yet it is the beginning of life and the beginning of wisdom. I have to illustrate that to you of course. So in the beginning, to talk on the problem of choice, let us start with what choice we do have.

In self-knowledge we always begin with ourselves. The first thing that manifests as yourself in the world is your body. So we must have a look at what choice you have in relation to your body.

You are born, without choice — without choice as far as the conscious mind that worries knows. So mind had no choice when you were born. In the body that is born you also have no choice in maintaining the breathing, the circulation of the blood or the continuous function of the vital organs, nor in the reconstitution of the body as the cells continually disintegrate. In fact, the body continues on its way despite you. No matter how much you, your conscious mind, want to change it, you can only do so very rarely.

There is a simple explanation for this. Your body is run by your unconscious mind — unconscious as far as you are concerned, that is. And you run your life with your conscious mind. The unconscious mind is the most powerful — it really is the superconscious mind, not unconscious at all. What it says, goes.

The unconscious mind contains no error. It can be reached sometimes by hypnosis, when an alien will appears to plant in it a suggestion that leads to the breaking of a body or a mind habit. This only serves to emphasise its tremendous superiority over the conscious mind, which rarely has the resolution even to give up a simple thing like smoking. The superconscious mind does not accept these suggestions either unless it gives its prior acquiescence.

Nothing the conscious mind decides to do to the body is enduring except in a destructive way. And if it does choose to try to change something it forgets or tires of the effort. The subconscious mind never forgets.

Another thing you will notice — looking within your experience as I speak — is that the only time you worry is when you have a choice to make. When you have made your choice and are in a state of choicelessness you feel a sense of freedom. It might be that you have only chosen to admit you were wrong, to get something off your conscience, but the feeling is unmistakeable. The state of choicelessness here is the state of freedom. This may sound fundamental, but in self-knowledge we deal in fundamentals.

Our question is: When are we mostly unhappy? The answer is: When we are faced with a choice. It is a time of conflict, indecision, worry. It disappears when we have chosen. When there is no choice to be made, and you are not aware of one, you feel secure. Choice divides you and you become the conflict of the alternatives.

Man's desire for more money than he needs is a striving to be free of choice. He imagines that if he had a hundred thousand pounds he would be able to choose as he liked, make mistakes with impunity, live in a dolls-house world where his incapacity would be overlooked.

It is the threat to our self-interest, the possibility of loss, that puts the barb in choice for us. We hate it, even though we do not know we do, because it limits us. You will have to look closely at this within yourself.

And now I am going one step higher, and you must try to follow, for we must always strive upward. The body-consciousness of man is the animal consciousness, the consciousness of physical force. This consciousness fills its limited needs and desires by brute strength or the threat of it. That which satisfies its body is its idea of heaven, and the heaven that it will get. When man was confined to that consciousness and he wanted someone to satisfy his body desires he took them by force.

Next, man entered the mental consciousness where he became aware of choice. This was the dawn of good and bad, and the beginning of his systems of morality. Mind would call it a higher state of living, but really it is only an extension of the other. Instead of depending on physical force, mind puts the emphasis on mental force. As the body-consciousness seized the bodies it wanted, so the mind-consciousness tries to seize the minds it wants — hence man's insatiable desire to be loved or liked or respected or obeyed. These are aspects of the desire for power and all of them carry with them satisfaction — the mind's index of happiness.

Above mind-consciousness is the consciousness of understanding. This is reached when the nous of man tires of desiring power over minds and objects outside itself. It turns its attention inward and strives for power over itself. This inward turning has to be preceded by a period of relative quietude in the desire-being.

Remember, the direction of the striving has to be reversed. And before you can go the other way in any medium you have to apply the brake and then stop. This is done in man by the desire to be a good man becoming dominant in his consciousness. A good man is a man who tried to avoid intruding on other men. He sincerely believes he wishes the best for them and in fact finds himself going out of his way to help others when he can. You will notice that this attitude is the beginning of self-denial. It is a purely mechanical brake on badness whose essence is self-assertion. The third stage of man is the stage of wisdom. It is above a good man. And before that he has to have been a bad man. These are the unalterable stages of man's evolution and development.

To become a wise man, the good man has to be destroyed. Wisdom does not recognise good and bad as the mind below imagines it. Wisdom has a morality of its own — an enduring one. Good and bad is the morality of mind, a shifting morality, because mind deals in opposites. Understanding, the third stage of man, is a world of unity, a consciousness of its own where opposites have united into an unimaginable harmony. It has a morality of its own that by the miracle of life, when it is lived fully on the earth, translates mind's cruel inconsistencies into a merciful justice.

You will remember that last week I pointed out that the morality of mind brought out of Christ's teachings the iniquity of the Inquisition. It justifies the slaughter of war while it prays for peace, says no and does yes, mistakes compromise for justice.

Mind's justice is a rigid thing. Yes and no are not rigid, nothing is rigid. Mind itself is not rigid — it is rigid only in its attitudes and grooves. The universal aspect of mind shifts in time, as style and fashion. Morality varies in Turkey and England because knowledge varies. Where knowledge is different attitudes are different and morality has to be different.

You people are coming out of this confusion by self-knowledge into the certainty of understanding. This certainty is an amazing thing that you must be experiencing while I speak. When I say something that you have not thought about before, but you know to be true, you will notice the certainty of your conviction. It would be laughable for anyone to try to tell you it was not true, you wouldn't even bother to argue about it. This is the power of understanding. As we proceed you will find yourself inwardly nodding agreement. After I have been speaking for ten or fifteen minutes you will notice yourself saying 'I know that, yes, that's true' more often. This is because you entered this room on the surface of yourself and the first ten minutes or so had to be spent in quelling your conscious mind, settling it down, taking the opposition out of it so you could listen with your understanding.

Every newcomer to this teaching wants to argue, has a hundred questions and a thousand opinions to put. But mind cannot stand up to understanding, for the understanding in a person, when they are ready, quickly recognises a source of itself. It surges up through the being like a great thirst that paralyses the mind of opinions and lies there still, listening with knowing delight. All the argument vanishes; even the questions are forgotten or no longer matter.

I don't have anything you do not have, except conscious self-knowledge. I have the same understanding as you within me, but I have seen it with my conscious mind. I would not be able to speak for very long to your conscious mind. It requires knowledge and I am sure you are much more knowledgeable than I. What I tell you is already within you. All I do is pull together the little areas of your self-knowledge and make you see them with your conscious mind, give you the realisation of them. You then have a greater nucleus to look deeper into yourself and your life, and a greater potential of realisation.

When you know yourself you know all mind; mind always operates the same. Man thinks there is individuality of mind, but there is not — not when you stand back from it in understanding. Understanding is above the individual mind consciousness, looking down. As soon as man begins to go into himself he has glimpses from up here — he starts to see the discrepancies of mind, and it worries him. He wonders why a good man cannot be good all the time. He sees himself being bad and it pains him, not the action so much as not being able to understand why.

Obviously everyone has choice. The point I have made is that you are at your happiest when you are choiceless.

If you personally have no choice, whose choice is it that directs you ?

Let us look at it together. Mind believes it has a choice. Is this true? Yes. You had to come to the meeting tonight.

But we will have to go further back than this to understand the question. Let us approach it from another angle. I say that the only thing man can do is to become conscious. I say — and you must not believe me — that his only choice is 'Will I become conscious?' If he does not realise this choice he remains unconscious. Anything that is unconscious obviously cannot have a choice — choice is synonymous with a conscious act. So man as he is does not have choice if what I say is true.

Let us keep going. Man lives his life in a state of unconsciousness. He is never aware of himself except for say a minute a day. An example of being conscious is when you suddenly become aware of yourself talking too much. You see yourself objectively as the others are seeing you and you realise you are making a fool of yourself. It is a brief, intense moment, filled with self-knowledge. You are conscious, and in that moment you stop talking. The fact of your observation of yourself brings about its own instantaneous result. You stop talking, you stop being mechanical. You do not choose. Choice is the deception of unconsciousness.

When you are conscious you are unable to behave in any way that is unacceptable to you. So how can you say you are conscious when you do things you later regret? You are either unconscious when you do them or unconscious when you regret them. So the only choice man has is to stay conscious or become conscious. There is no other choice. As unconsciousness is man's natural state, his only choice then is to leave it.

How do you make this choice? Is it a choice? Isn't it really just an act of remembering yourself, of observing yourself, of becoming conscious of your actions and your thinking every moment. Does it require choice?

No. There is no choice . . . only awareness. The deliberate way to become conscious is through the practice of self-observation. My teaching is that truth corrupted into method and system.

I would like you to observe yourself at this moment sitting and listening as you are. You observe with your attention, not with your eyes.

The moment of awareness is gone even as it begins and you lapse back into identification with your body and the distractions of thought. Identification is limitation and unconsciousness.

Remember that being conscious cannot eliminate all body's and mind's apparently stupid actions. You, the new man, is freed of them but their essence and function is mechanical reaction in a mechanical world. To abolish their unconsciousness completely would be to end the world.

To become suddenly conscious of ourselves in everyday life is always a bit of a shock. Take the person who becomes self-conscious when he does something in public and feels the attention of everyone turned on him. It becomes an agony. He is so unused to observing himself that he doesn't know how to perform normally while he and everyone is watching. If you are familiar with yourself you cannot become embarrassed because you know exactly what other people are seeing. You know your stupidities and they don't shock you.

When he sees stupidity in himself, man tries to make excuses for it or sweep it under the carpet if no one is around. He will go to extraordinary lengths to cover up the truth about himself. If someone has witnessed his foolishness his first action will be to find someone to tell the story to, and distort it so that when he asks 'What else could I do?' the person has to reply that he did the only thing he could do. And then he feels better. He refuses to see himself as he is.

Some people love having others look at them.

Yes, but that is an outgoing, not an ingoing. They are performing with the deliberate intention of being observed. If they are observing themselves, it is as the performance not as the performer. But if they are caught unawares, where there is no performance, they too will become self-conscious. This is true of the greatest actor until it is time to begin performing.

Isn't the result of this hypercritical state of observing yourself a complete separation from this world?

How can mind and body separate from this world?

Well, you cease to value anything that goes on in the world. You cease to talk to people, you cease to go to the party at which you were embarrassed. You would cease to be a person living and doing the normal functions of life.

What are the normal functions of life? Going to parties? Why not?

But why do you have to be a fool when you can eliminate much of your foolishness by observation. Is it bad if you see something foolish in yourself and you wipe it out? Obviously it must be good, or you would want to perpetuate your foolishness.

It would not be fair to say man chooses to cling to his foolishness . . . or would it?

What is individuality?

To spend your life chasing money is certainly not individuality. Everyone does it.

To be happy and unhappy, sad and gay, angry and kind — that's everybody, not individuality. To love your children or your sweetheart or your mother; to dislike those who offend you; to hate or kill the enemy; that's everybody too.

Individuality must be something else, if it exists. Perhaps it is what remains when man rids himself of what is false in him. Perhaps it is choicelessness. You must see for yourself.

How many times have you been conscious since I mentioned it? Not many, if at all. You forgot. What chance do you think you will have of remembering yourself when you are reacting mechanically to your environment? Or when you are being dishonest — and I'm not talking in terms of stealing pencils from the office; I'm talking about speaking ill of another man, of betraying another's trust, of being angry. This is all dishonesty to yourself, unconsciousness.

If you are angry you cannot be conscious, nor at the moment of talking maliciously about another. All these negative reactions are false and cannot stand up to self-observation. They wilt, and die.

You think you choose to be angry? You think you choose

to be honest? No. Man mistakes reaction for choice. You may as well try to argue that the earth chose its orbit around the sun. The earth's path is the product of several diverse mechanical forces. So are man's actions. He begins to free himself by refusing to yield to reaction, to absorb the blow or force, to deny himself his outward going, his self-assertion. He succeeds by being conscious; all the problems go.

Where there are no problems there is no need of choice, and choicelessness again is the state.

I worry, but I don't choose to.

Let us look at worry in relation to choice. Worry never has an aim, therefore it never has the intention of action — it deals in ifs and shoulds — imaginary choices.

Planning has aim, but you cannot plan and worry; you are too busy planning the action. In planning you go from fact to fact. Do you choose? No. You have your aim and you use the fact best suited for your purpose, just as you jump from stone to stone in awareness when your aim is to reach the other side of the stream safely.

What is man's aim?

Man does not have an aim. That is why he is interested in impressions. Worry deals in impressions; aim deals in facts. Man has aim when he has a job to do, and he deals in facts or he would not get it done. But he has no aim for himself — so most of his life he worries about impressions.

What is right and wrong?

Right and wrong is morality. It depends on self-interest and knowledge.

If someone sees a man in the street slitting open a child's chest with a knife he might scream 'Murder!' If he had a gun he might shoot the man. But if he had known the man was a surgeon carrying out an emergency operation he would be sorry he shot him. He would regard the surgeon's action as good.

The basis here of course is that it is good to save life. But is it good? We might be mistaken. If we had more knowledge we might see it is bad, or that it does not matter.

Man thinks it is good, and in the absence of greater knowledge we must assume he is right and live by the tenet that it is wrong to kill. A child might point out that if it is wrong to kill it is wrong to go to war. Killing is either right or wrong or you don't care. If your morality is that it is wrong to kill a man then it is not right to kill him for any excuse at all; not even in self-defence. But try and not defend yourself. It doesn't work; nor does man's morality because it is a compromise with his self-interest. It is a lie; and the lie is in the idea of choice — in the unbelievable delusion that you can choose when it is right to kill a man and when it is wrong; or when it is right to be honest or dishonest.

Choice is the creator of both honesty and dishonesty. Choice is vanity; the only evil. Honesty is choice plus pride; dishonesty is choice plus guilt. Both are the judgement of ignorance.

Surely war is different. We go to war to protect our families.

Do you? War is death and destruction. You go to war to kill and destroy. Your reasons are your justifications for your immorality.

Are you saying everyone who goes to war is immoral?

Of course — if he believes he is moral.

Are you amoral?

What's that ?

You don't believe in morality?

I don't believe in anything.

Is war wrong?

What is war? Where does war begin? War begins in the individual. Every time you lose your temper you are at war. That is where war begins.

Man says we must eliminate war but his hope is as foolish and insincere as his morality. He cannot eliminate war until he eliminates it in every single man. He has to begin with himself . . .

What can man do?

Be honest. Be true to himself. A man should say 'Yes, I'll go to war I'll kill if I have to'. Does he say it is wrong to kill? No. But he does say 'I, and I alone, will decide for myself when I will kill and when I will not kill. I do not make a rigid rule for myself; I have seen myself break the rule too often. Even when I have decided in advance that I will be a coward it is in the moment that I have turned and fought. I will leave it to the moment and look within myself'. Then man will discover a new life, a new freedom — action and decision without the corruption of choice.

You are obsessed with choice. You choose incessantly. You make a thousand useless decisions a day that you are not entitled to make and do not have to make. You read the newspaper; ninety-eight killed in a plane crash. Isn't it terrible — that's a decision, a judgement, a choice. It has nothing to do with you that ninety-eight people are killed, but you live off this artificial emotion of choice that this is good and this is bad — of someone else's tragedy. What does it matter to you if ninety-eight strangers are killed? There are also ninety-eight people being killed in Vietnam at this moment.

Why don't you find that interesting? You don't, or it wouldn't be just one paragraph in the paper. Three Britons among the dead the headlines scream. So what? Only that you choose to regard yourself as a Briton; you limit yourself and limit your interests. In Vietnam there are Vietnamese and American dead. In America that will make the headlines. Can what is important depend on where you choose to live, or which newspaper you choose to read? Surely what is important has more substance than that. Surely it is beyond choice.

If you confined your ceaseless judging of what is good and what is bad to events which actually affect your own life you would make tremendous progress towards freedom. You would make the astounding discovery that the rest doesn't matter, that if you never read another newspaper in your life you wouldn't miss anything really important — only the earth's most fertile source of opinions and dispute. So where do your decisions lie? In the things that affect you; and there lies your duty, not your choice.

Has it ever struck you that men have been killed since recorded history, and tomorrow or the next day there will be another plane crash? Men are going to go on dying and dying. What does this mean? Is death good? Is death bad? Or is death just a fact? Is death life?

Well, it is a part of life. All that we see within our consciousness is a part of life. Death must be life.

You obviously have to refer to something.

Where do you refer ?

Well, to yourself.

Yes, but not to your mind. If you refer to your mind it might throw up the ten commandments, one of which says you shalt not kill. You might have to kill. Can you be true — professing one thing and doing another?

How do you know there is something there to refer to —an absolute thing that will tell you how to act in this world. How can it tell you how to act in this world if it is not part of it?

Who acts in this world?

I do.

Where would you expect to find the solution to how you should act? In what someone else says?

If I was an idiot or a madman, I wouldn't know.

But you are not an idiot or a madman. I'm talking to you.

Oh, yes.

That's where it is found.

I refer to myself. But what am I referring to; an accumulation of things I've picked up in the last twenty-seven years?

No, you are referring to understanding. Understanding is

49

always referred to in the moment of the challenge of life. It is imagination or mind you refer to when there is no challenge — no intention to act, such as now.

How do I know there is anything beyond that? I've had no sense of it, no indication that there is an absolute morality to refer to.

An absolute morality is a complete morality; there is no morality outside it. To recognise it you would have to put another morality or idea beside it. Then it would not be absolute. You can have no sense of an absolute morality. You must experience it.

How do I experience it?

Always in the moment. And you will notice that in the moment there is nothing there, only the action or no action.

All the mind does is organise the possibilities of the action out of the patterns of experience. It cannot decide the action — understanding does that, and chooses the moment as well.

Mind in this position is something like the accused waiting for the jury to return. It knows the possibilities of the response, but not the actuality or when. This is the period of indecision, anguish and torment that man knows so well. With the action comes relief. It is the mind that frets, not the doer, the understanding.

Why does mind worry?

Because it doesn't know itself; doesn't know its function.

You do not know the truth of what I am saying. You might believe it is true but that won't stop you being anguished and tormented, because I am giving you knowledge from outside yourself. You have to discover it as a living fact in your own observation of your own mind. Then you realise it. Realise the knowledge. That means experience it.

Realised knowledge is understanding, and understanding is freedom. You will never be anguished again then.

I do not understand. Are you saying we should kill or we should not kill?

I am saying neither. I am saying you must do your duty. And your duty is to do what you have to from moment to moment.

Is it a sin to kill? If it is then all the men in the last war are guilty of the most heinous crimes. Are you going to accept that?

In black and white, but there is this absurdity of life . . .

Where is the absurdity? An absurdity means there is something wrong with the way we are seeing things. We have to find a solution and that is what we are looking for now. Your earlier question was: 'Where do you refer?' The book says thou shalt not kill. But I have to look at life and say 'Obviously my parents did kill by supporting a war of killing. Now where does my morality come from?'

We are looking for a solution but there may not be one. We may be deluding ourselves.

Well, you are deluding yourself by thinking there is not, aren't you. You are living a lie by accepting the teaching 'thou shalt not kill' and then condoning killing. Why do you accept anything?

51

Because it affects me. Because I don't want anyone to kill me.

Why do we have to accept anyone else's morality? I said to you earlier that the reason you people are here is because you are good people within the definition that I gave. You cannot begin the process of self-knowledge with me unless you are a good person. I cannot talk wisdom to anyone who is still in the so-called bad-person stage of development. For the simple reason that they cannot understand. They are not ready. They are bored stiff apart from anything else. And besides, how could I tell them to look inside themselves for their morality? They would see only their self-interest and use my teaching as an excuse for their intrusions. At that stage of development man's point of reference is self-interest; the judgement of his mind. And to maintain some sanity in his world he needs the restraint of codified morality, the ten commandments, or the criminal law — anything that carries with it the threat of pain, the curtailment of his self-interest should he transgress.

You have been through that. You have gone beyond that. Your point of reference is within you now, in your understanding, which as yet seems to be nothing at all. But you dare to ignore your duty. Go against what you know to be right, if you can, and see what happens. See that within the wisdom of your own understanding sits your judge and your executioner.

What about children?

Children are the return to earth of understanding. Their understanding is incapable of full and efficient expression until the new mind develops adult intellect on which understanding can reflect. Therefore they need a fairly rigid rule of right and wrong.

But I have been amazed at how quickly and easily children grasp and can live this more abundant way. There is little opportunity of course. The world hands the child its absurd, rigid tenets and tells it they must be obeyed, while the adult world around ignores them. The child becomes cunning, as we all are, professes it believes, and does what it can get away with — the lie we call living.

The ultimate of your own morality is choicelessness. Once you have been a good man you will never again have to choose whether it is right or wrong to intrude on someone. You will never have to make that choice again.

The desire to be good is in you, but that is not enough. There is no such thing as good in relation to the whole; that is what we are trying to learn now. There the will of the whole *is*. You will find it is in the moment and in your understanding.

Wasn't Christ a good man?

If you like to ask me questions about Christ we will go round in a circle again. Because Christ was a good man and a wise man. All his goodness tenets have opposites, but all his wise ones have none. This is where his followers find themselves in conflict. If you strive to live up to his good tenets — all of them — you will end up with the opposite, like the Inquisition. If you practice his wisdom teachings — such as take no thought, do what you think to be right, die daily, pick up your cross and follow me — you will find you are guided.

You have to live wisdom. A good man says he will not speak behind another's back. A wise man says nothing. He knows he might. A wise man says 'I must remain conscious and observe myself'.

If you know something about someone the impulse to tell

53

others can become almost unbearable. The mind gets tremendous satisfaction out of being the first to report something. That's why an advertisement for one evening newspaper screams 'Be first to know'. It is pandering to this mind instinct. When we talk about someone we are obeying it. What do we enjoy telling? Mostly what is bad and scandalous. It has to be extremely good to be news. Gossip is our main occupation. Even the good man has to swallow hard to hold back what he knows about someone when the opportunity to tell comes. And usually, after a sly justification to himself, out it drops.

The wise man knows that while he lives in a world of mind and be-first-to-know this impulse is going to well up in him. He knows the only way he can overcome it is to separate and see its falseness, be a man and watch it dissolve. He then feels the silent strength of having been true to another and to himself. Did he choose not to utter it? No. He was choiceless. He became conscious, and when you are conscious there is no choice — you just observe. It is all done from within where you know what is right and wrong.

A new morality is born. You will notice that it is the Christ morality and the enduring morality that the good man strives for so fitfully.

Is it wrong to criticise, say the Prime Minister?

No. The Prime Minister espouses a political policy which he believes to be right. No-one can be certain it is right because only the future will show that. That which has to be decided in time is in the world of mind, the world of opposites and opinions. So there has to be an opposite to the Prime Minister and an opposite to his policy if what we say is true.

Opinions always contain the probability of being wrong. A

politician said in the paper today that next year will be a good year. You could find just as many reasons to contradict him. We won't know who is right until next year. So you are entitled to your opinion in that world while you think it is important.

I have experienced that I have no choice. But sometimes I think I have.

Then you have had a realisation of understanding. When you think you have a choice you are back in mind.

It is impossible for mind to see it has no choice. That has to come through understanding when the mind is terribly still. Man's mind is never still enough to realise it — at least not until he has worked on himself for a long time.

Why do I want to find out I have no choice?

You might not want to find out. So you will go on dreaming.

Don't I decide to sell my house?

No. It is dictated for you by events. You have to see this for yourself and I have told you how.

Man's choice is like a tin of worms. If you are one of the worms wriggling like mad you think you have a choice. But to the man in the great big world outside you are just a tin of worms. He knows what you are doing without even looking in the tin.

Is it choice to have pursued the same old things century after century? Surely choice, if it exists, is something else.

It is still living.

True. But it is not life. Living is relationship. That's all that is. Life is something vastly different. Life is the thing beyond living. Life has no relationship. Life is being complete in itself, and it is choiceless. Which means that eventually the life is lived so that every moment is choiceless. Man desires nothing outside the moment, every need is filled for him. There is no need of choice. He might be injured by a car you say. His body might be, but not him. All his possessions might be taken? That does not hurt him. He says 'I am not mind which recoils at information of loss. I am consciousness. I am complete. I am untouchable. I hear the song of life within me. I enter the state of love at will'. And yet, does he not perform in the world? Of course he does. He looks and appears to act like everyone else while he chooses to.

I still want to do other things.

You must do what you have to. While you occupy a body and a mind they will have to perform in the world. Body contains ego whose primary function is to protect body, as co-ordinator of sense-perception. So it has to perform while your body lives.

Ego is also the agent of desires. Our desires are what we are interested in. Only pain, or fulfilment or observation ends desire. Do what you want to. But be sure you are conscious while you do it.

The knife has to be a knife. It cannot be a spoon. A knife's consciousness is facing the fact it is a knife. You have to learn to be yourself.

First, you have to face the fact that you are what you see you are. Then there is the possibility of change. Not before. While you are making excuses for yourself you are not being yourself. You are acting. Putting on personality, being what you are not.

Do not be alarmed. When you finally see yourself as you are you will find you are only looking at the shell of what you used to be. You will be looking down, for you will have risen without moving.

What is desire?

Who desires? We do. We are desire.

Is desire wrong?

Desire is a fact. It cannot be wrong. To be unconscious is wrong for man. So to desire or act unconsciously is wrong for you. If you observe your desires as they arise and as you are about to perform them, the unintelligent desires will collapse like all the other negative reactions under self-conscious scrutiny. What you do while you are conscious is what you have to do. Sometimes it will shock you.

What did you mean when you said we are desire?

Man is the action or the stress between the object wanted and I, is he not? He is not the I or he would be able to satisfactorily explain why he desired the thing when he is going to die and leave it behind anyway. Desire is all he consists of until he becomes choiceless and desireless. But by then he is the I — and he knows the answers.

Because man is desire he is happiest when he is striving. But when he has many desires they pull against each other and he feels split, which he is — and listless, because his energy is diffused. This is the state of boredom and mediocrity of most men and women. They desire so many passing and superficial things that they don't know what they want. They have no aim and very little delight. And too many choices.

A man who strives with delight is a man with an aim. The fewer the desires the greater the energy and the greater the zest. If he can desire one thing he can achieve the impossible — he can become conscious. How many desires are you?

A man with one aim, of course, is choiceless. He is the happiest man. He relates everything to his one aim so he never has to choose, never knows conflict. If he has two aims he has to choose and compromise between them all the time.

I'm not sure about being happiest when I am striving.

The question is: When are you happiest? Let us look at it.

You are happiest of all in the state of love. First, it is choiceless; you could not stop loving if you wanted to. You make no decisions, you just are. As soon as you think, the experience of the state of love withdraws. If you are with your love you just sit there fulfilled and desiring nothing. But it cannot last, because it has an object. The loved object has to pass on or die. You are then unhappy and out of the state of love.

Love is the desire to become one with the object loved. So love is that striving. How can it be a striving when it is such a placid, motionless state? You cannot become one with an object; the closest you can get to it is to eat it and let it pass into your system, but that does not satisfy your desire for love.

How about sex? Sex satisfies sex and body in a way, but it does not satisfy love, the striving for unity.

The terrible fact is that man's love is a striving for the impossible — the union of objects. The partial physical contact that takes place is for the satisfaction of body and the desire of sex, which is the fourth thing in man. The living together is the satisfaction of the mind's love in the form of knowledge of possession and various other aspects of imaginary power. But what about man's love, the delicious striving that is none of these things? How does it ever get its fulfilment?

Man's love, what he is striving for through his countless lives is for love without an object, enduring, never-ending union with his own higher-consciousness . . . the other way to the loves of this world which he continually identifies with. When he achieves this final union he loves all things, for the one consciousness is the same in all minds, all bodies, all desires and all matter.

When else are you happiest in your life? When you are meeting a challenge wholehearted, one-pointed, choiceless. If you are doing something because you feel you should, you have chosen to do it and there is very little delight in it. If you are engaged in something that does not delight you, you can be sure you have no real aim.

A condition of turning inward is that nothing every really delights you anymore. Striving outward comes in spurts and you begin with great zest . . . but the importance of the aim dissolves, and you wilt. Nothing will really delight again at this stage until a teacher comes and puts you consciously on the way. This way has no aim, for you cannot desire what you do not know. Yet it becomes your entire life. You are then the striving for what you do not know yourself.

I think I am happiest when I achieve.

That is the state of choicelessness.

You can't have it both ways. When you achieve and are happiest you sit back and for a little while you are choiceless, are you not? But will you stay in that state? Good heavens, no. That is heaven and you can only stand little doses of it. You would go mad. Very quickly you will choose another challenge, become another striving.

You had better have a look at it, hadn't you?

Some strivings are not pleasurable.

That does not change the fact that man as he is, is a striving. Whether the striving is pleasurable or not is a secondary subjective impression.

I said man as he is is happiest when he is striving, because that is himself. The state has no opposite except choicelessness and that is the constant happiness of the man he has yet to become.

That which causes the greatest happiness will also cause the greatest unhappiness. That is the law. So man's strivings have to give him the impression of pleasure, displeasure or indifference. That does not alter the overriding structure of man as he is. He is at his unhappiest when he is not striving, when he has nothing to do.

Is it right to be indifferent?

You cannot cease being indifferent so it must be right.

You are indifferent at this moment to the light switch and your bank account. Man lives for himself so he seldom notices the significance of indifference. Happiness and unhappiness are for himself, indifference is for the rest.

You will understand this better if you are able to observe that everything lives off everything else. Everything has its own positive experience. Remember, we are the tin of worms, each contributing to the experience of the whole. Our indifference creates the opportunity for another to know pain or pleasure, or in turn to be indifferent.

You will notice the triune. There is always the triune if you can see it — the equivalent of good, bad and indifferent in every single act of creation.

It is the observation of these things that makes man see a life outside his own limited interests. He begins to see a totality, a greater vision that eliminates him in its immensity yet contains him in its necessity. This vision is the experience of immortality.

What do you mean by immortality?

I cannot tell you. It cannot be communicated by knowledge. It has to be experienced.

When you die and find you have survived death you will not experience immortality. You will experience that you exist by the conflict of some relationship. But immortality is beyond relationship.

Mind cannot know immortality, but by becoming absolutely still, by becoming nothing, it can experience it.

When are we creative?

When we love what we are doing. When it is no effort. When we can whistle a tune or sing a song without interfering with the action; when we can laugh, speak to the person beside us without feeling a disturbance; when we are not concentrated; when we are relaxed; when there is a harmony between what we are doing and every sound and movement about us. We are then efficient, happy and creative.

The mind cannot create. Creation must be new or it is not creation. The mind cannot produce the new; it draws only on the past out of memory. The images of mind are a reaction of the past, a synthesis of what is old. It is a modifier, a reactor, a re-furbisher, a renovator and re-arranger, but it cannot create the new.

Mind always tries to concentrate. It is the only love it knows — limitation.

You still have to concentrate.

No. The word is meditate. Meditation cannot be disturbed. Meditation is a background of freedom that the creative person has to create first. It is the opposite of concentration.

Concentration is an attempt to deny the right of existence to the moment of life around you. It would exclude, like the cell door, instead of absorbing, like the breeze.

Concentration is the opposite to creation. Concentration says 'This thing is all my life consists of. Stay out, dog that wants a pat. Stay out song, stay out child, stay out noise, stay out life'. That's not beauty; that's not creativity; that's not loving what you are doing.

The energy of meditation is attention — a different thing altogether. You attend on the subject and that brings into your mind all the related facts at your disposal in your memory. The background state of meditation means the mind stilled so that attention can be complete without the usual irrelevant, undisciplined mind-ramblings coming between and making it necessary to try to concentrate to keep them out. Meditation is freedom.

I find creativity a state of bondage. You have to concentrate on listening for something to be transmitted to you.

I was coming to that — the state when man is waiting to create.

Every person who ever creates, whether it be song, poem or a design, has to first of all go into a state of meditation. It brings about a state of stillness (how I will explain later) and it puts the mind onto the thing you want to do. If you want to make a new piano obviously you cannot be thinking about writing a poem. The attention brings up knowledge out of memory and understanding out of experience. And they all lie there together waiting — poised and listening and still.

Suddenly, out of the silence, out of the beyond, into mind comes the fact, the refreshing new that sets the rest of the poor, mediocre, concentrated world agog with its beauty, its brilliance or its genius.

Anything new has to come through in silence in this way. Man is so seldom still that he does not notice it, but the creative man does. He knows the essence of his brilliance or his genius is not of him.

What if I don't know how to meditate ?

To study and do anything is to meditate on it. Your expertise will depend upon the love and effort you have to put into it. Love mostly, because there is no effort in love. To the degree that you love the subject the subject loves you and this is transmitted as intuition. Intuition is another form of understanding.

All this is meditation on the subject. Its combined result is that whenever you direct your mind onto the subject, the mind goes still. You can direct it along any relevant channel without fear of distraction. When you want only awareness and understanding it lies alert, awaiting your command.

You will notice how different this is to the undisciplined way it performs in your personal life. That is because you have not meditated on yourself.

What is creativity anyway? There's nothing new under the sun.

Isn't there? The creative man seems to think there is. But perhaps this is just man as the striving in reverse. Having been given the fact, the new, his delight is in the striving to bring it into the world — instead of being the striving to possess the world.

Is there really anything new?

Let us say there is nothing uncreated. That which is new is only the discovery or release of it bit by bit; another word for time.

Nothing can come before its time, not even the solution to a problem. A problem denied its solution is the creation of striving. A problem united with its solution is nothing, or death. Life to most men is a problem.

You must have wondered why a solution occurs today and not yesterday. If you look back, you people who are beginning to search for wisdom, you will see every solution occurs at the right time because if it had not you would not be here tonight. If you are sincere and reach for this work, you will see the path of so-called accident, chance and coincidence that led you here.

Why man must suffer

IF WE ARE GOING TO UNDERSTAND SOMETHING we first have to be able to stand back and see it exactly as it is. There is no other way to self-knowledge.

You do not necessarily need a method but sooner or later you need help to consciously realise the knowledge that you have. That is my function.

What is truth? It puzzled Pilate as it puzzles every person who thinks about it. Yet it is very simple. Truth is the fact. In the world, an illustration of the fact is a red light when you are driving. It is a fact that means stop. You can ignore it or obey it, see it or not see it. It does not change the fact. That example is knowledge of a fact outside yourself. Self-knowledge, of course, deals with facts about yourself.

Wisdom is the ability to impart the fact so that it is understood. If someone is going to teach you to drive a car he has to be able to impart to you the fact that a red light means stop. If he cannot, he has no wisdom as an instructor and is no use to you.

A fact unimparted or not understood is truth — either in the world or self-knowledge. For instance, all the facts that you need to find freedom are in the New Testament . . . but they are hidden there as truth — the unimparted or the not understood. So man cannot find freedom through it alone. Only wisdom can free a man, truth cannot. Truth is within, wisdom comes from without. And the greatest wisdom is every moment of your life.

The most difficult things for man to see are the facts about himself. He sees only what he imagines himself to be and that is an amazing concoction of falsehood. From this unreal viewpoint he gets an absurd impression of what life is about.

Man can seldom look at anything unless he refers back to memory, to what he has been told or read; someone else's theory. Very seldom does he ever go to his own understanding because, imagining himself to be what he is not, he is never quite sure what he really understands. When he refers to memory he refers to that second division of himself, the mind. Memory is of mind, and no mind ever contained wisdom — only worldly wisdom. And worldly wisdom always has red lights and green lights, stop and go, yes and no. And unfortunately they do not mean the same the world over.

Out of such confusion comes the wisdom that justifies the paradoxes and inconsistencies that man finds himself expressing as 'I believe'.

In the search for truth we don't believe anyone or anything. We do not have faith in anything. But we listen and we look within ourselves and say 'Is that true or false in my experience?' While you listen tonight you will find yourself saying 'I know that is true'. It is your understanding working. But if you refer back to mind, if you want to quote the Buddha, you will find a complete opposite to everything I say — and I'll be able to find a complete opposite to everything you say. We will get nowhere. But if you like to ask me questions in relation to self-knowledge I will give you an answer that has no opposite. Truth has no opposites; that is the fact.

I said man imagines and uses impressions instead of facts. The hardest thing for him to see is the fact. The way to see the fact is to listen without going back into memory, but it is not easy.

I talk to you before questions to get you into a state of stillness for listening. When you come in from the outside world your mind is busy with the stimulus of things outside yourself, a momentum that keeps it judging and going back even unconsciously into memory. After a while, because we are one-pointed here, you find there is an absence of thinking, that the mind goes quiet, and you enter a state of awareness that needs no memory to operate. This is quietude. It is only in this state that you can listen and discover.

Why must man suffer? First of all we must understand what suffering is and what happens when we suffer. I am speaking of mental suffering. What action takes place in us? Is it not a feeling of insecurity, the taking away from us of a direction, a state or a thing we are familiar with? Or more dramatically, the removal of a source of knowledge? If my mother or my wife dies, why do I suffer? Because I am deprived of a source of experience, a continual supply of information that affirms my existence as a relationship. The more exclusive the relationship the more intense is my feeling of being insecure and the more I suffer.

What I am saying is either a fact or not. The subject of these lectures is to present life to you from a different aspect, to help you see behind the emotion that is yourself. If you look at the world through Christianity or any teaching that is old you are going to look at it in an orthodox way. No matter how hard you try you will find yourself getting into grooves and theorising on what is the right way and the wrong way.

I have told you there is no such thing as good or bad in yourself; that a wise man can never be a good man and yet he embodies a morality that is far beyond the expectation of any good man. I tell you these things even though they may be outside your experience so that the potential of your vision is always wider — so that when you are walking down the street and something happens to you, instead of looking at it in the traditional way, out of your understanding will eventually come the ability to look from this new direction. You do not have to worry about the opportunity occurring, because wherever truth is ready to be revealed in a person, life has to illustrate the fact so that it can be realised in the moment. Life is a totality that speaks to you through all things including these lectures and then provides you with the experience, if you are sincere. Sincere means you are ready to listen to life and watch it working outside your self-interest.

Change is pain. Suffering is pain. So suffering is change. The smashing of the dropped glass is nothing more than what would be its cry of pain if it were conscious. Man imagines, because he has a conscious frontal feeling, a consciousness inanimate things do not enjoy, that pain is felt only by him and the animals. But we have to look at life from the total aspect if we are going to understand it, not from the narrow individual one. We have to look at what happens to the individual I from life's point of view. We cannot expect to see this tremendous totality from the limited interest of a personal self.

Looking at it that way, change is pain. The motor-car tyre that screeches as it rounds a corner is in pain. The difference is that it does not have what we call a sensitivity to pain, an apparent consciousness. Wherever there is change there is friction, and there is pain.

What is this pain? Obviously from the analogy of the tyre it accompanies a changing of direction. Man, as mind, always wants to go in a straight line. But the fact is that life's direction is elliptical, and that is why we say mind is our greatest enemy. Mind always struggles against the fact of change — like man's morality which in straightline-thinking says it is wrong to kill. And then, when man finds himself about to be killed, suddenly it is acceptable to kill in self-defence. And then he gets a fit of conscience because it is wrong to kill.

This pain of conscience is no different to the pain of the whip on the bullock's side, saying go the other way, change direction. In the beginning the bullock, and man, both need quite a lash to turn them in the other direction. But after a while, if the man is intelligent, he begins to realise the pain is only there while he refuses to yield. When he is headed in the right direction, when his attitude is right again, he always finds the exciting new — even if the pain has killed him.

If we look at pain and suffering as a desire for life to change our direction we start to learn new things. For instance, we might learn that death cannot be dreadful.

When I was a newspaper reporter I saw people weep over death a thousand times. It occurred to me, 'Why does everyone weep the same when someone dies?' It is distinct suffering is it not? — undeniable pain. Then what are they doing that is wrong? Why are they not yielding? There must be a lesson I thought.

It seemed to me that life was a totality in which all things including death must be right and good, if only man could see it. It seemed to me that if man was reacting to an everyday occurrence like death and it was painful to him, it must mean he was not realising something, not listening, not going in a right direction. Later I saw quite clearly, as you can, that death is good, a magnificence, a thing of beauty. If there was no death we would stuff the planet until we couldn't move. There would be no green lawns, because if man could not die then certainly the grass could not.

But in his arrogance, in his conceit, man thinks he is more important than anything else. Of course he is not. As an individual, the way he is, he is nothing but a potential. As a species he is magnificent. It is for this excellence of the species that the individual is searching. But he searches in self-interest from the narrow point of view and not as the species which is the totality. The species is quite prepared to die as individuals and sees nothing in it. It knows there is nothing wrong with death, that it is something to be yielded to with outstretched arms, once it is inevitable.

So if man would only look about him he would see the monster he would create if he could eliminate the death he mourns so often, his absolute annihilation as a body-being. If he could see the fact he would know the answer to the question 'Why do I lament death when someone near and dear to me dies?' After all of history's dying he still watches others weep and tomorrow will do the same himself.

Man is knowledge. Without knowledge man is nothing — nothing that he can understand now. First we have to see that we are knowledge, plus the desire for more knowledge, a struggling pain to know.

Knowledge is all we want. When we lose, suffer or know pain one certainty you can look for is that a loss of knowledge is involved. And when we are happy it is the gain of something — knowledge. When we are indifferent we are secure — in our knowledge that what we possess is safe.

All this knowledge comes into the mind through the body. We call it sense perception. It is a very real world. And it is all we have while we identify with the body and its tenuous relationships. How can we be sure there is something else?

We have all known love. Its incomparable intensity of experience, its freedom and its light-heartedness. The beauty of a sunset, the smell of the forest, the touch of a hand, the sound of music, the taste of cool water. Would you try to tell me that the man who is paralysed, deaf and blind is denied the experience of beauty and love because he has no sense perception? Can beauty and love, our highest experiences of excellence, be so superficial, so exclusively limited? Or is the need of objects in which to experience beauty and love our own unconscious limitation of them and ourselves?

Love and beauty are not knowledge. They are experiences

in the moment in yourself. They do not come through the senses any more than you experience yourself through the senses.

You have to use pain as your teacher. No-one asks you not to weep or mourn. That would be a suppression, a limitation. What you have to do is to observe what is happening, what has gone. And you might observe that the intensity of the great loss you feel diminishes with time. You might even wonder why, if you felt you could die with pain of loss yesterday, that it is not so urgent today. If you feel in your despair that your life has ended, be true — and die of your grief.

You have to challenge life like any other teacher. You have to say in the midst of your grief 'Life is teaching and I must learn from it. I'll know this grief and I'll experience it because it is a fact my mind is tied to this object as a source of knowledge to me, which I am identified with by interest and proximity. But I recognise the existence of my mind and that its being is emotion and that the tears that flow are the inevitable operation of mind and body in this world. But I am not my mind, and while I weep, because I look, I demand that you — life — show me the truth of my suffering.'

This is separation in the midst of pain, and this is suffering properly — demanding of life its solution in the midst of your agony. Not becoming identified with it and saying 'I'll die, I'll die'. No. You are a man or a woman and you have tremendous strength when you separate into your understanding and hold on.

This is the reason for pain and suffering — to sort us out so that nothing can ever touch us again. And while it is going on you will hear your bewildered mind appealing to you, saying 'I want to know what is happening, my whole world is crashing'. And your consciousness will say in silence 'Hold on, I am here. The secret of life is death and in that is life's integrity. I am here inside of you. Hold on little mind, hold on to me'.

Eventually the mind says, 'Oh yes, you are my strength' and it surrenders to you and you are then a man.

You have implied there is a force that guides man. Is this so?

What is man? Look for yourself and answer yourself. Look and see if there is a path that has brought you to this moment to hear these words. It may be a tortuous path, but it will be distinct if you are sincere.

Can man give up if he wants to?

Can you? Can you opt out of being a part of life? Death is a part of life. How will you give up?

This path . . . the search for self-knowledge . . .

Life is the search for self-knowledge. The points you see as marking a path are the limitations of your understanding. The man who sees a path has more understanding than the man who does not. But what is it a path through? A path through life? There is no path through life. There is only life.

There are turning points.

There appear to be. You change your job. Your family life changes. Later you see the significance of the change and say 'that was a turning point'. But what you are looking at is a tracing in your memory of the body's movements, altered circumstances. What you cannot remember is the change that in the moment occurred in your consciousness. This is going on every moment, the mind only remembers the dramatic, the obvious. So it sees a path instead of a totality.

What is realisation?

When do you realise anything? When you suddenly understand. It is a moment of amazing clarity, is it not? Those moments when you realise you have been a fool; when you realise you are no longer in love; when you realise you are no longer afraid. These are the moments of tremendous change in us that bring about the real changes in our lives.

You will notice that it is not the mind that realises. The mind is always astounded by the revelation, as though it were an astonished observer. This is because the impulse comes from within, out of the understanding which lies behind the mind.

The mind is like a mirror, constantly reflecting or reacting to events outside. This is the superficial body-mind existence that man identifies with and finds so frustrating. Unknown to mind, every experience it has generates an energy not known to science, that passes back through the mirror into the real entity in man, his consciousness. This energy is understanding. I am not using the word figuratively, it is an actual energy. It builds up in different cells in the brain which together represent the totality of the person's potential experience. A man realises something when the energy of understanding reaches a flashpoint and irradiates or enlivens a part of a brain cell. The flash of inspiration illuminates the mind from behind and it is momentarily stilled with amazement. It then goes about actuating the new knowledge in relation to the body's environment and our lives change significantly.

The realisation of a fact like this is the moment of truth that the world glibly talks about. It is yours for ever. Never will it change, never can it be lost.

Is it the unconscious mind?

It is not the mind that is unconscious. It is us. I would term it the superconscious mind.

Is it God?

Of course. And the more you realise it, the deeper you will go until you go beyond God, for want of a better word, which is still God, or 'X', or yourself.

In realisation, which is changing of your understanding, there is no suffering surely?

Suffering has to precede understanding. You cannot understand until you have experienced.

I have been dealing with pain but of course the triad comes into it, on the broader scale. The triad of man's experience is pleasure, displeasure or indifference.

If you win a hundred thousand pounds the experience will obviously give you some understanding. Man will apprehend the win as being pleasurable, because it is gain. Whenever man thinks he has gained he is happy, but frequently he gives himself the wrong information. He thinks something is a gain but it is not.

Usually, in the way of things, to gain in relation to self-knowledge, is to lose. Man's idea of gaining carries very little experience with it — except the pain or worry that it inevitably brings. His winning puts him to sleep because there is no pain.

The time when self-knowledge really comes is when you suffer. The opportunity for the man with the money comes afterwards when he has to justify his refusal to help others, defend his change of attitudes, experience the greed or understanding of his friends. Here is pain and self-knowledge.

Suffering changes us. Good things put us to sleep.

How can you reconcile the differences in pain of a similar thing happening to two people — to a man who is just one of the masses and to another who is an individual striving towards understanding?

Everyone is progressing towards the realisation of total understanding. When I say the masses have no hope, that only the individual can escape . . . there are no masses, except in the individual's imagination. Everyone is an individual, but only to himself.

Total understanding is not achieved in one life. It is realised at a point in one life but it is the steady accumulation of the experience of thousands of lives. Take the man who has led, say, two or three lives. His suffering will be dictated by a consciousness that is focused on the body and its five senses. The man who has had a thousand lives will have risen, through suffering, above this limited consciousness. He will have entered mind consciousness, which is mental relationship with objects beyond their value as a comfort for the body. This is obviously a more subtle form of power — knowledge — vastly exceeding the previous limit of satisfaction. But the greater the potential of satisfaction, the greater the potential for suffering. In this way does developing consciousness contain its own spur.

As I understand you, suffering is failure to disidentify with the mechanics. In relation to emotional suffering I see this. How do you see physical suffering? I cannot see physical suffering as explained by your thesis.

I have been dealing with the comprehending thing which is

man's mind. This is a good question because it is going to take us down out of mind into body. To do this you will notice we will have to leave the ego behind.

Ego is the thing that suffers when we experience psychological pain. The ego's existence depends on its ability to find reasons for everything. You will never suffer psychologically without the ego providing you with an object for it. Eventually however, when the ego has been battered and weakened sufficiently for self-knowledge, it begins to grasp that in the higher ranges of consciousness suffering *is* ... and needs no object.

In physical pain, say an accident or surgery, where there is no inflictor to blame, the ego experiences impotent bewilderment. It is a pathetic state we have all observed in suffering man and animal. The innocence of it, the absence of knowing and comprehending, in fact the absence of ego, arouses in us the higher feelings we know as sympathy and compassion.

So to understand the answer to this question we leave the judging entity of ego behind and try to look objectively. To do this you have to use the total viewpoint I mentioned earlier and not judge, but try to observe the fact.

Physical pain is the sudden return to its source of the energy of creation. Creation — growth or formation — is a pretty leisurely progress. But wherever there is pain there is destruction. It is this enormously concentrated backrush of energy that produces the sensation of pain.

Remember the law of physics that says matter can neither be created nor destroyed yet may be changed from one form to another. The same law applies to energy because matter is energy. So if you appear to destroy matter — smash your hand with a hammer — what you have done is to turn it back into the original energy and the instantaneous conversion is pain.

Looked at from another angle, pain is the crossing of the

desire to live. Here again you have to rid yourself of personal identification and look at the totality of life, or you will not grasp what I say. For a thing to exist there has to be a desire to live or be in that form. When you cut my body you cross the desire to live in that form and I feel pain. Now come up to the mind level and you will see the same process there. If we cross your desire for anything you will feel frustration or pain.

This applies to all things not just to man, though we might have to find another word for pain. When man destroys the atom and produces the world's mightiest explosion, matter is destroyed and rushes back to its source in an ecstasy of energy.

Where is the source?

Where is your source? Self-knowledge is the search for it, is it not?

You say all things are going towards self-knowledge. I do not understand this.

Take the body. We are not aware of its comprehension of itself. We are aware of ourselves in it, as reaction. We are not aware of the body's continuing experience from moment to moment, the build up of hunger and all the other processes which is its joy of living. We are the reaction that says, quite suddenly 'I'm hungry' and goes and gets it food; or 'I'm going for a walk' and gives it exercise. We are the dramatic reactions, but what about the thousands of moments that go on unobserved by us every hour; the waving of the hands, the crossing of the legs, the swallowing, the wagging of the tongue, the movements of the head, the standing up, sitting down, the never-ceasing action. What is that expressing itself without our participation? The body-consciousness — an

77

entity just as real and distinct as you who call yourself I.

This body-consciousness is proceeding towards self-knowledge. Not the form, but the consciousness in the form. Our form is frontal perception but that, as I explained in the analogy of the mirror, is only the appearance and not the consciousness that is developing as understanding behind.

The body-consciousness, to us, is inconscient, but it still exists, as it exists in all forms. When the body is hurt its consciousness goes through a transforming experience of life just as we do through pain, and it gathers understanding or knowledge of itself.

Self-knowledge is the realisation and release from a previous limitation. So consciousness by this whole process is always moving up, continually shedding the limitation or identification with the form it previously took to be itself.

In the same way, this floor we stand on must have its experience of life or pain. Pain at that level appears as friction or heat, because wherever there is life, inconscient or otherwise, there is heat, and wherever there is heat there is change. When metals melt, when wood burns, when the lava flows and when the rose grows, consciousness moves ahead, for life is nothing more than conflict in harmony.

Where does the mind and instinct come in?

Mind-consciousness begins in the basest substances of the creation — rocks, metals, etc. Instinct is simply mind's desire to live in whichever form it occupies. It appears in the beginning as the law of attraction and repulsion and as the electrical cohesion of the atom. Mind-consciousness progresses through the elements to the plant kingdom where the desire to live manifests itself as a 'live' force. Here, also, is the first suggestion of 'intelligence' — the organism grows towards the sun, its roots turn away from harmful substances.

Mind-consciousness experiences the animal kingdom — bacteria, insects, fish, fowl, mammals etc. — during which the desire to live expresses itself in mobility and development of the senses to protect the more complex organisms. Instinct, here, reaches its optimum and begins to account for the entire operation which is quite mechanical. It is during this stage that there appears to be individuality of consciousness, say in the dog. But this is not so. It is all done by the universal mind functioning as instinct. That appearance of individuality is simply individual knowledge memory — imposed on instinct.

At the point of man — lowest man — individual consciousness does occur but remains latent for tens of thousands of recurrences while instinctive mind develops fully as conscious mind — that is, mind capable of knowing the entire universe but not itself.

Individual consciousness — the next stage — begins to assert itself by mind turning inward and seeking self-knowledge. Mind consists of memory plus desire which is endless activity. The inward turning gradually eliminates useless thought and finally purifies the mind into a state of stilled alertness. It is then illuminated from behind by the blazing energy of its own fully developed consciousness, and it realises it itself is nothing and never was. That God, beauty and everything else worthwhile was always within itself; that they are itself; that it is immortal and that to the degree it does not exist as trying and wanting, it is God the creator and sustainer of the whole creation, and that there is nothing outside of it, never will be and never was. But most beautiful of all to me, is that it sees the secret of love.

If a finger is cut off, the body suffers the pain but the mind suffers because it knows it no longer has a finger.

Yes, loss of knowledge. That is a correct separation.

Let us deal with the mind first. The body's suffering is reflected in the mind by nerve experience. The whole body exists in this way in the mind, because body is a product of mind. In other words, the whole body exists first as a neurological structure in the head, then in the flesh. Cut off the hand and it still exists in the head and so the limbless man can feel pain in the absent fingers. You will notice that in all this ego is absent.

Now let us deal with the second part of the question — this is where the ego appears — with the knowledge that it will not have the finger any more. I am incapacitated. The knowledge of incapacity is man's greatest agony. The cruellest thing you can do to him, the greatest hurt or insult, is to draw attention to his incapacity, especially emotional or psychological incapacity. He hates it, because all men know they have it. What man is searching for is his real capacity or his real self.

The loss of any object or state, to the ego, is a loss of capacity to assert itself. So it usually reacts by blaming someone, worrying or just suffering.

Doesn't the body miss the finger?

Doesn't the man miss his dead son? The body will adapt. So will the man — eventually. But who will curse or weep or pray? Not the body, but the ego. If there were no reaction, only the understanding of death, there would be no ego. And perhaps what would remain would be a man.

What does the body want?

The same as you, surely — to be secure, at ease. The difference is that the body-consciousness, because of its limited capacity for experience, has a limited capacity for satisfaction.

What is security for your body? Enough food, warmth, air, rest and exercise. What is security for you? We don't know really, do we? There seems to be no limitation to what we do or want. While we are secure we feel we don't want much at all, but the slightest little setback keeps us awake all night. And we have so many things to lose — our family, our possessions, our prestige, our job, our friends, our money, and a thousand other previous relationships we cannot even imagine until they are threatened. Only at the moment of parting do you know what you love.

If I suffer a setback in my work, I suffer because I realise I have been deprived of something; that there is a loss of having-ness. I know for a fact that the effort to disidentify with this situation reduces the suffering, but if a man walks about with a duodenal ulcer and is in constant physical pain, just how this is related to havingness I don't see.

It is related to havingness and separation. The havingness he does not have is comfort. He wants to be secure in health. The pain is the reminder of his insecurity — his ill health — just as psychological pain reminds us that one of our external relationships is insecure or threatened.

Now what is the reason for pain? We have seen it indicates change in matter. It has another very important function — it is a signal to us that an opportunity exists for a change in consciousness, if we can separate and suffer properly.

Physical suffering is a tremendous opportunity for self-knowledge but a very difficult one because it lessens the ability to disidentify. Still, because it is difficult it is tremendously rewarding in results . . . but only after a period in which you seem to be working for nothing.

This is the way of things in all suffering for self-knowledge.

You were talking about losing the game. I don't think you explained it properly because I feel you can lose the game by becoming incapable of making further effort towards realisation.

Yes. It means you will put something else before it.

I mean a total loss of the game, in all lives. If for long enough you fail to push it you are finally unable to.

No.

You said in your first lecture that only certain individuals would in fact win and the rest of them would completely lose.

You misunderstood what I said. I said that for the masses there is no hope, that only the individual can escape. I also said this group has no hope. But the individual here has. Who is the individual? You must answer that.

One can lose the game in a sense of one life, and one might lose it for many lives. Obviously, to have thousands of lives we must be rather dilatory, mustn't we? But the great movement of all consciousness, which includes all individuals, is forward. So you cannot lose.

You can lose it by becoming not-man.

No. Once you have reached the level you cannot go below it. You cannot even stay where you are because every moment you are not the same. The whole creation changes every moment, always moving forward in the understanding of itself.

Alleged authorities are absolutely contradictory on this.

What is to lose? It is a concept of conscious mind which dies after seventy or so years.

Only that which dies can talk of losing. What can immortality lose?

Your arguments are from mind.

Mind goes on to heaven, though, you said. That must be immortality.

That is not immortality. That is survival, a dead state for the still dead.

Immortality follows the realisation of death not the sterile knowledge of survival. If you know you live this moment and when your body drops you still know you live — what is new, what has happened? Nothing. Immortality is the new. Can you contain the new in what is old?

The idea of survival is the best good that mind can imagine. So it survives to enjoy its limited heaven. Then when the entity returns to shed more limitations, the mind, not having found immortality, dissolves. And another personality mind develops with no memory of the previous existence because this would direct it along an old course — and life is always fresh and new.

The memory of all lives remains in the superconscious mind, but it is withheld because until man is total understanding he is a creature of habit and he will revert to the old. Understanding is expanding experience, not repetition.

If understanding can gain something it can also lose something.

No. Understanding does not gain. Understanding is. All

the understanding in the creation is in your consciousness at this moment. Consciousness is symbolised or represented in your head by brain cells that lie dormant until awakened by the energy of realised experience — understanding.

I have said understanding as consciousness is the recurring entity. The mechanics of rebirth are that in the new brain the cells enlivened in previous lives are born almost awake and require minimal experience to set going. This experience coincides with the development of the intellect so we sometimes find amazing understanding or wisdom among the young and unsophisticated.

Understanding cannot lose. What is it then that man loses with such pain and reluctance? His ignorance?

If I lose something how is it ignorance?

Ignorance is the apprehension or fear of loss. There is no doubt the object goes from us or is destroyed, but our ignorance lies in our clinging, our incapacity to see that every moment is a going of the old so that the new can come. Understanding is the diminution of this attitude.

The mind is the sole supporter of ignorance — it deals in becoming. It is always trying to become rich, or humble, or wise, or popular or intelligent. Its 'isness' is its wavering moods. It is happy, discontented, bored, pleased, angry, and when it loses it is loss. Understanding 'isness' has no fluctuation so it is secure in itself all the time. It knows that loss can only exist in relationship. Where there is no relationship there is no desire, only the fact. And that is love.

I do not understand absence of relationship.

First you must understand relationship. This opportunity is given to you every time you lose. It is very difficult because mind exists as relationship. And the more you understand, the more mind, as comforting activity, begins to disappear, or die. It gets frightened and confusion begins, terrible confusion sometimes. Unless the person has a teacher he can go almost insane. The feeling of nothingness and emptiness is appalling. Sometimes he even doubts his own existence. Why? Because the security of mind is its endless activity and curiosity and when these things are being replaced by desireless-knowing there appears to be nothing but void. In void there is no relationship. So this void is love.

If you love something you have to have a relationship.

When the mind loves anything it cannot bear to let it go. This tension between the mind and the object is relationship. It is a bond of desire, distinguishable because it always imposes a limitation on the freedom of the person loved, in the form of expectation. Its tragedy is it can be a one-way bond which is cruelty. Such love, even though it is shared, contains lust, no matter how high the mind would try to put it.

Love has no relationship. This means it puts no limitation on the freedom of the object loved. If the object or person goes, it goes because it must; for love knows love would never go unless it had to.

And why does love go? To love and to learn, for love without relationship is life's energy and learning is the reason for life. Learning when such love as this is understood is the raising of individual consciousness to the pinnacle of life's endeavour. The consciousness becomes love incarnate.

Does this mean a man and a woman of high consciousness can never really be certain of staying together?

Love without relationship is its own certainty. The

85

movement of bodies and objects is the certainty of the moment . . . two worlds, one consciousness.

What exactly is understanding — understanding of what?

Understanding of what life is. What else is there to understand?

Why do you understand yourself then, and not life?

You cannot understand life until you understand yourself. If you don't know whether the knower is reliable how can you ever be certain of what it sees or records? Is that not your problem, now? You are not certain of yourself. Your relentless discontent, your wanting, your trying, are but your own uncertainty.

Life is certain. You are the uncertainty. Know yourself.

Can the scientist understand life?

No more than you do. He is just as uncertain of himself as any man. His certainty is in a knowledge of something outside himself — just as you are certain of how to do your job or drive a car. You can be certain of all the intricacies of mathematical method, describe all the laws of the universe with it, but it won't help you to understand death, to experience immortality, to be certain of yourself when you close your office door and are just a man.

What is evil?

Evil is death. When you apprehend evil you are in the presence of something seen or unseen that represents the possibility of death of your body, a desire, a memory or an emotion.

Man has many deaths for eventually he has to die to his body, to all desire, all memory and all emotion. Fear of the loss of a person or thing is the apprehension of a death that one day you will have to suffer. All things go when we die. But the going of people, things and states while we are alive is only the procession of death that is life.

What man must do

WHAT MUST MAN DO? You all know the answer to this by now — man must become conscious. Conscious of what? Conscious of himself. What is himself? Himself, as he is now, is habit. Habit is the negative side of him that makes him live a mainly negative life. Habit is his unconsciousness.

When man is compassionate, really grateful, when he is helping others unselfishly, in all these moments he is conscious. They are the positive parts of man, and together they represent one state which is the state of love.

You will remember I said — and it provoked a little doubt — that the state of love is a state of no thought, a state of being. Compassion is the same as the state of love although it might be apprehended in a different way. The basis is the same — no thought, an outgoing of yourself to another being whether it is the person you love, the person you feel compassion for, or just a stranger in the street. It is not an outgoing of your opinion or your advice; these are helpful, often necessary in the world, but we are not speaking of that. We are speaking of an outgoing of your being that has no need of words, and this has a tremendous effect on the understanding of the receiver and the giver.

That is the positive part of man, the part strangely enough that eliminates him, annihilates him, and yet he does not resent it. He never resents the state of love and yet he is never less of a self-assertive being than when he is in it. At the same time he never enjoys a greater delight. People continually say to me 'You teach a way of annihilation of the individual but what guarantee have I that I won't become a vegetable?' Well, any of you who have loved will know the answer to that question.

The negative side of man is habit. This is the thing that man has to become aware of, by separating. You will recall that we said separation is standing back and looking, because the knower cannot be the known, the looker cannot be the looked upon. If you observe yourself thinking, it is the higher part of your mind observing the lower mechanical part. In the same way, the part of you that observes the body cannot be the body.

Habit is of body and of mind. What you have to do is observe your habits of talking, thinking, moving. You will find the observation eliminates a lot of 'bad' habits. It cannot eliminate all because man has to be 'bad' as well as 'good'. But so long as he is conscious of what he is doing he is safe. If you are conscious of being bad there is a greater possibility of your being able to overcome it at its source. But if you sweep it under the table by justifying yourself you have no hope of ever overcoming it.

What man must do covers twenty-four hours a day and I cannot deal with it in an hour or two, or indeed in a hundred hours. It requires continual instruction and practice. It involves meditation which is essential before man can become conscious. Most people meditate anyway, but they don't do it consciously. And it requires contemplation — an extension of the idea of meditation, which man should aim to experience continually. These, plus observation of himself — in the beginning, observation of his body movements — make up twenty-four hours a day of work.

We will start with body habit. The body's habits are not bad. The body is like a child and we should treat it as such. It has to be looked after and if we injure it we are not doing our duty. The body's habits, as I said, are not bad ones, but they are terribly material and binding to the earth. They are a wonderful springboard for us to bounce the mind off.

One way to begin the momentum of separation is to observe the position of your body whenever you can remember to do so. Do not change your position. The object of observation is not to change — if you change your position you will select another position. Who will select? The mind; the very thing we are aiming to control. So we cannot allow the mind to interfere.

Man's constant delusion is that the mind can change the mind. It is why he fails to overcome his bad habits and always fails to attain consistency in his idea of goodness. You have to go beyond mind, and the beginning of the beyond is the observer.

What happens with self-observation? You just look. If the way you are sitting displeases you will change it without having to make a decision. You won't have to think; you will just move, because by the way of things you will not tolerate anything that is unacceptable to you while you are conscious.

Man seldom sees the position of his body. If you observe how you are sitting now you will experience how difficult it is to be the observer even for a couple of seconds.

The idea, of course, is for you to reach a state of almost continual separation. You will have to watch very closely to see the tremendous subtle difference between a decision of the mind to change a body position and an action of the body consciousness which changes it.

Try to separate when you walk along the street by observing the way you walk. This sounds elementary I know, but the hardest part of separating is to remember to do it. So try to use every movement and action as a reminder. Most people have been observing themselves on and off all their lives, but to be of real value it has to become a regular conscious action.

Notice that perhaps your left foot turns in a little more than your right; that you tend to slump along; see how your arms swing and the speed you walk at. There are a thousand new things to observe about your body. It is a trick, because while you are looking at your body you cannot be identified with it. Our worst habit is identification with the body and its relationships. When this happens we don't know what the body is doing and we are unconscious of it and of ourselves.

At the dinner table observe how you spread your butter, how you hold your knife and fork. You do it all by habit. The idea is not to change habits or for anyone to tell you what is right or wrong; that is not necessary. But how often do you look at things like this?

A way to break any body habit is to substitute another action for it. We usually slump back to sleep into the old habit, but you can break any habit if you become conscious often enough by separating. It is not a bad idea to do things in a different way. You will notice how insecure you feel when you go to a new place until you get some habit into it.

There is nothing wrong with habit. Man is a creature of habit and it would be as wrong as it is impossible to break all body habit, for it plays a big part in our survival. But you must separate mind habit from body habit. Mind habit is the enemy. An example is when you say good morning. There is nothing wrong with going through the terms of courtesy. It is essential with such self-interested egos as we are or we could not live together. But having said 'good morning' you will notice how often you have to go on. If there is a silence the atmosphere is almost desperate. Man finds silence very difficult. When you say 'Good morning' in the lift everyone else says 'Good morning'. How many can just stand there? The lift-driver cannot; he has to go 'Phew' or whistle or say

'Great day isn't it?', and in London in the winter you get the same conversation every morning.

It is quite automatic because people cannot bear the sound of silence. Try saying nothing if there is no need to speak. Stand silent and you will probably feel very uncomfortable.

All this is breaking the unconsciousness of habit. From now on do not tap your fingers on the desk; it is habit. Do not cross your legs or tap your feet unless you have deliberately decided to do so. Then go ahead by all means. But if it is done without your conscious knowledge your body is actually doing something without your consent. These little habits are a tremendous help to separating.

Strange things happen when you separate. You are assisted by one half of the totality, but the other half is trying to drag you back into unconsciousness. The scale will always come down your way if you are sincere. The number of times you can separate today will help you tomorrow. Every time you tap your pencil it is a little alarm-clock saying 'Wake up, separate'. You have to listen for the alarm-clocks, they are ringing ceaselessly. Man seldom hears them in his busy-ness and denies himself this consciousness that will lead him to step back and become the master of his universe.

You cannot master the life around you until you have mastered the mind, then by the miracle of life you are the master of your life.

We now come to observation of the mind or thought process. This is harder, but because it is harder the alarm-clocks ring louder and you are a little more uncomfortable.

The mind is reaction — anger, irritation, viciousness, all those sort of negative emotions we are watching for. As soon as you can after the reaction begins you have to try to stand back and watch it. You will only get a flash of it at first — then you will go back to sleep and identify with it. That is our habit. It is however sufficient to become conscious of it while it is working, then the reaction will start to wilt. Eventually, during let's say anger, you will actually see your little body-mind machine performing as the reaction while you look on from within, another being.

Do not identify with the reaction because it is not the real you. The reaction is completely mechanical and habitual, it is part of the machine which we all are. To try to stop it is to join it and identify with its origin. If the reaction is unacceptable to you who is watching it will collapse. No negative emotion can stand the piercing, exposing glance of the real you unless it is function, and that is another story.

You start to treat this reacting thing in you as your enemy at first, then later as your other small child. It is then no longer permitted to perform without your conscious assent. This is a sort of humility to yourself which you will understand when it happens.

Do not regard it as a humility to anyone else. We don't want humility to anyone. Conscious man does not need it. By being humble to himself he is humble to everyone and everything. Mind does not know what humility is, it only thinks it knows. Humility is an actual part of the higher separating entity.

The best alarm-clock for reaction is pain. Every problem encountered in self-knowledge contains its own solution. The problem in man is pain; the solution is separation. There is never a solution outside the problem.

Men have used the deliberate self-infliction of pain as a means to separating. It is not our way but that does not mean it is not someone else's way. Some men expose themselves to dreadful physical agony and as a result experience a death-body separation in which they find themselves outside their body. But this is not what we want. The death-body separation is completely mechanical in that death comes to all and it is experienced eventually by all. To experience it before death is like a preview, a tantalising, unsatisfactory thing. What we want is a separation while we are on earth, a permanent thing that makes us the master of ourselves here and beyond death.

When you feel injury it is the loudest alarm-bell ringing. Strangely, if you can separate, the pain will remain as intense but somehow will be a little more distant. Another thing you will observe is that if you stare consciously at the pain it starts to break up. You must experience this yourself to understand what I mean. Its basis is that nothing false can stand up to the glare of consciousness.

Pain you might say is not false and it certainly is not when you feel it. But there is a falsehood in it and if you are able to look upon the area of pain within yourself some of it starts to break away because some of it is false. The false part is fear. When you take the fear out of pain you remove some of it.

Fear is false and fear cannot stand the constant observation of your separated self. To fear you have to think, and to separate you cannot think. You have to be in the now to separate and fear can never be experienced in the now. Fear is always experienced in relation to the future. What is experienced now is an excitement, an awareness.

If someone is running at you with a knife you do not experience fear. How many men have explained 'I didn't have time to think? Thinking is our enemy and imagination of that type is our enemy. In the moment of awareness, when the threat of death or injury is upon you, if you think you will probably be killed. Thinking is too slow. At the moment of threat you need to use the higher apparatus, self-knowledge, which is understanding. The body reacts instinctively and that is body's understanding — the lower part of mind.

The other understanding is where you have to use the mental process without thinking, where you have to act

95

quickly to get out of the way of the knife-man — you stand back into your understanding and you become aware in the now. You don't think. You look, sum up the situation and you just act. You might get killed but at least you will know you were not afraid.

Are there any questions?

Can you recommend some books to me. I think books can be useful because they are the accumulation of past wisdom, and perhaps you could also explain if and how there has been a thread of wisdom throughout man's history picked up by certain men.

I find that I usually have to recommend books for the individual. When I speak to a person I am usually able to pick up their need. There are several books that I could recommend. There is a man called Krishnamurti, and if you have started to grasp what I talk about then you will understand Krishnamurti. There is Gurdjieff as reported by his pupil Ouspensky who can be useful. Joel Goldsmith can excite the reader so that you hear the music of it all, but not the work that is required. No teaching is the same, but they go in the same direction.

One of the things I have not touched on so far is God. I do not usually speak about God because God is something we have to ignore until we can experience God, but a tremendous thing for those that have experienced it. Any philosophy that teaches you about God first won't get you there. You have to experience God and then God certainly will get you there.

The mind cannot experience God. It cannot know God. It can imagine it does and it can have all sorts of experience such as jumping outside the body and looking down at itself in bed asleep, but it is no closer to God. But, as I say, some people have experienced the love of God. If I said to you individually

'Have you ever felt that you loved God?' The reply that I find I usually get — and people are extremely honest and humble when they are sincere — is 'I don't know'.

If you have experienced the love of God you would know. The number of people who have experienced the love of God in the world is very small. Once you have experienced the love of God at the intensity I am speaking about, it is the end of you. You are finished. You may die very quickly. It is a tremendous vibration, an absolutely disintegrating power. Many people have an awareness of God, but that is rather different.

However, I have to say this about this particular teaching. It never leaves the world. It deals only with you, and you can apply it twenty-four hours a day. And when you get your freedom and self-knowledge it will happen now, and while you are not free you are not free now. Everything happens now.

I am not qualified to go over other teachings but I promise you that if you start to grasp this teaching and you work hard you will be able to read great words like those in the New Testament with a new insight. The things that you have heard repeated for years, the things that you have mumbled by habit in church, suddenly have a new meaning.

Christianity is not understood. It is a way of annihilation. Every teaching that is worthwhile has as its basis annihilation of the seeker, but the mind cannot imagine what annihilation means. The most important parts of Christianity are never quoted . . . those that deal with the annihilation of the individual.

The individual is never really destroyed. All that is destroyed are his opinions and his judgements. Once you eliminate these you look out into the world as an individual, with individual responses and individual feelings, but at the back of you there is a join with totality. So in a sense you are one with everything and in another sense you are an extremely aware individual. It is not elimination of the individual; it is the elimination of his clinging.

Man's mind clings to everything; never happy unless it calls something 'mine'. You have to get rid of the fences by a conscious action, by becoming aware of the fences of the mind. You can only become aware of what is false by observing what is; and by observing what is the false falls away. When you get rid of the fences you get rid of your chains.

What is time and how is time linked or related to the thread of teaching since man's beginnings?

You cannot know what time is until you have become one with everything. It doesn't matter what man wants to do, no matter how far he progresses with science, he cannot know what time is.

Time is an eternal mystery — for the mind. It is not a mystery to those who have experienced oneness with all things. When I say one with all things, this does not mean the table can become one with the wall opposite. This third thing — consciousness — that I keep talking about is the one thing that is one with everything. There is nothing outside it except form and it is the very essence of form. Mind thinks in terms of space, but even in the depths of this space there is still something like one atom per cubic yard of space — but of course that is only what scientists have discovered. There is no space, it is only something that man has not yet been able to name.

You do not become one with everything, but you have the realisation of oneness with everything. And if you are one with all things you are one with this space. This is a very real experience of the mystic — to experience oneness with the space between two objects. When you become one with everything there is no space. Space is eliminated. Space is the condition of time. It means 'I am an individual and there is an object there'. Therefore it is going to take time for me or my consciousness or some pulse that I send out, to get there. But if am the object sending the light I am the light and I am the space and I am the object there. Time is eliminated.

I have said all things are one, all things are a totality, and once you realise the totality you eliminate time and space. Time and space are the condition of the mind world. So, that eliminates the world — you are out of it. This description is incommunicable; all I can say is that you have to experience it.

The scientist, you see, has a problem that the metaphysician does not have. The speed of light is 186,000 miles per second according to the scientist. If I am in a spaceship travelling at half the speed of light and I send out a signal which travels at the speed of light that signal should travel at one-and-a-half times the speed of light, but the scientist has found that nothing can exceed the speed of light. The scientist has found an extremity of the creation as far as he can probe it. He keeps finding these gaps, but they are precise gaps.

Consciousness is a gap. The mystic death is experienced at a precise degree of self-knowledge. It has to be experienced. There is no law about God's grace or that sort of thing. If there is a God he has fixed that precise point and as soon as you have that self-knowledge you have to go through a certain death.

The scientist has found at the other end that he cannot find the square root of two. There is a gap.

You said that one part of the totality tries to pull you down and the other half tries to raise you up?

Yes. The idea of the creation is that the creation must go

on. The creation is composed of continually burgeoning knowledge. This way is a destruction of knowledge, a destruction of complication. When you separate you find you are no longer interested in the complication of life. One of the complications of life is worry; that which makes man worry about an event instead of acting.

Worry is creation — the creation of problems, arguments, conflict, and it spreads its waves of creation. But that which does not worry spreads nothing. Worry exists because ignorance exists, and ignorance is the basis of the creation, and ignorance continually complicates or creates. Complicates is only another word for creation. That is why you can start off any enterprise and it will become complicated. The creation's job is to continually create. Death wipes it out, but knowledge goes on and complicates for other groups. Knowledge is the complication of the creation continually being manufactured. Man identifies with this knowledge and thinks it is important. Some of it is, most of it is not.

One of the achievements of this way is to know what effects you and what does not. News is gossip. Gossip is impressions — based on false impressions. Anyone who gives up reading newspapers for a few weeks starts to find he doesn't need them. So the creation's job — or the universal mind's job — is to continually dream up ways of complicating everything, and when it is complicated enough, wipe it out and let the knowledge remain. This is life. Death comes along and wipes out man's form, but the knowledge remains. What the man did, how he affected people, stories and impressions, all lovely complications. Then it wipes out the society's life, then the generation's, and all the history books, and on it goes.

Just to make it a little more complicated, we have a war. Man finds a superficial reason for the war. He is completely inconsistent. War begins with anger within the individual.

Eliminate that and there will never be another war. But there will be of course because if all men became like that the creation would start to diminish — and that is not the idea.

Everything gets complicated because the universal mind wants it to be complicated. The way we are teaching, you start to lose interest in the stupid things of life that you used to identify with. You start to put your vision on your inner-self: you start to meditate; you go silent.

Is the ultimate aim of the work non-being?

No. The object of the work is to serve within the world. The idea of the work is to free the individual so that a sufficient number of individuals can remain free to retain the knowledge of freedom in the creation.

Man's motivation — and the reason for existence — is the knowledge that there is something worth living for. The striving is trying to find it. Looking outward is the creation. As soon as man turns inward the individual starts to destroy the creation.

When anyone is ready they must, by the law, find a teacher. You will notice that if my words have interested you, you feel that here at least is something you want. Here is something that does not depend on knowledge of books or anything like that.

You say that moments of effort to self-remember or separate in the course of the day are preserved for the following day. It would appear that the accumulated process would get easier. In my experience the process is entirely the reverse.

The creation is composed of waves and they are going in all directions, and man strangely enough is purely a meeting point of several of them. In the beginning of the work it is easy. You cannot come to the work unless you have developed sufficient self-knowledge for understanding to be expressed or realised. In coming to the work the accumulated self-knowledge is brought to the surface. It comes together and you say that this is what you want. It is then realised over a period of time in the world. But unfortunately in the material world everything is done a little by trickery and this is no exception. It is almost as though that were to get you in. You get fine results; even have spiritual and psychic experiences to begin with. And then comes the arid period. But you will find that you cannot have these periods when you are with a master. You have removed yourself from a master. You removed yourself or he removed you from him because periods of suffering or dullness are good.

A man has to be helped otherwise it is like a man trying to pull himself up with the handles of a bucket and both his feet in the bucket. Everything is mechanical — even what I say to you is mechanical in relation to higher states; in relation to lower states it is wisdom. But to the degree that I can help you, to that degree do I progress. I have to progress too, and I am in it for myself. I have to give, even if it is to one person. To the degree that I raise you so I am raised myself.

You here will be able to teach other people who do not have the same understanding that you have. It will be your duty to help them because you will find that wherever you go in the most unexpected places someone will ask you a question and before you know where you are they will be listening. But be careful. There is such a thing as 'guru-itis'. It's a terrible thing to discover something that is the hope of the world; it is so wonderful that we want to share it with others, we want to give it to them in all humility, but it is not that easy. You cannot give it unless they are ready.

Also, you have to have something to protect you so that you do not make a mistake, go too far and find you cannot answer questions. This protection is provided by not going outside your own experience. You can teach anyone at all as long as you stay within your own experience. Do not teach anything outside your own experience. Talk as much as you like . . . within your experience.

While you are teaching or talking with anyone you will notice that you are able to stand back and look at yourself talking. You will always be aware when you have accepted the temptation to go outside your experience. Sometimes you will ignore it and you do so at your peril. Say 'I do not know'.

To the degree that you give to them so you are raised. After you have spoken truth to anyone, within your own experience, you will come away with a feeling of delight in you; a real excitement. You have given the one thing that man can give; you can give nothing else. If you give your money you give of your body. If you pick someone up you give of your body. If you give your opinion you give of your mind or your experience.

The only real giving is that which will free man of worry and mental travail. But unless the person is ready do not try. And how do you know they are ready? Let them ask. Never tell anyone anything until they ask. That is your protection. When a person asks they are in a state of humility and they will listen.

Observation and meditation

I WILL TALK FOR A LITTLE WHILE and then invite you to ask questions. The questions should be about yourself and in your own experience. We do not talk outside our experience because out there lies intellectualism. We do not use opinions. The basis of this teaching is that a thing is either true or false — or my understanding is too limited to allow me to understand yet. You do not accept anything I say to be true unless you know it to be true in your own experience.

I have explained before that the mind is the divider; the mind is the devil, the mind is the enemy. When you leave this meeting and get into the world you will swap your opinions and the mind starts to divide you from the source of the teaching.

In the beginning the source of the teaching is myself and the degree of understanding that you have within you. Eventually you become the teaching and there is no need of me. That is what we aim at — full self-discovery.

Only he who knows himself can be a teacher and only he who doesn't know himself can be a student, although even the person who knows himself is always a student to a higher master or a higher knowledge.

In this teaching we deal with three aspects of ourselves, naturally and arbitrarily decided. The first is the body whose servers are the senses; the second is the mind whose food is knowledge; and the third is the supporter of yourself, consciousness — a thing rarely experienced by man. Its food is understanding. We use everything we have to know ourselves, because we are everything that we have.

Beginning with the body, you might look at yourself now — I don't mean with your eyes, but with the inner attention that is you — and you will see the way you are sitting. There is no need of course to ever change what you see. As a matter of fact it is an error to change your position immediately because to decide to change anything is a judgement of the mind. Later on when we start to observe the way we think, if we allow the mind to judge, it will be the mind judging the mind and we will be trapped in a vicious circle.

It is very difficult to hold this state of observation because after a few seconds you tend to become identified with your relationships and your environment, and you are then unconscious. Don't think you are conscious; you are not. You are completely mechanical, a pawn of life, buffeted from here to there by many forces. It is in the state of unconsciousness that you know the pain and suffering of worry and limitation. If you are able to hold separation, not just from your body but from your mind, you are then free, out of the world, but still in it, and you are untouchable. That is our object.

In separating from the body you will see how it works and performs mechanically. Then, by a deliberate action, you may choose its position. If you observe yourself walking round-shouldered you watch for a while and then by a deliberate decision make your body walk as you want to. You need not think you are going to cure yourself immediately of walking round-shouldered. Our object is not to cure the ills of the body but to become conscious. But as a by-product of this you will find you get far greater control of your body and that mechanicalness starts to drop away from you.

The mind is a creature of reaction; it lives off reaction. Without reaction it dies — that is, goes quiet and still. All the world loves an active mind, but little does it know that the active mind can never be wise. The mind itself can never be wise, it has to become still, mastered by the self, and then through it can shine something else — your higher consciousness, which is what you must become.

One reaction of the mind that we are after is anger. You will recall that I said that we are helped here by a law of life; a law that man does not understand because he is always looking at things outside himself. The law is that if you observe something that is false in yourself it will start to wilt and disappear.

There is no anger and us; when we are angry we are anger. You cannot separate while you are anger, but as it gets towards the end of your anger, you will find that to the degree that you have devoted yourself to this method you will be able to separate and see the tail end of it. Then your duty is to trace it back, see the source, and when you understand it you will see it is false. To the degree that you see it is false it will start to drop away, and you will never ever get angry again.

But do not confuse that with the right of even the most conscious man to appear to be angry or indignant. That is a different thing and we have to remember that while man occupies a body or a mind on this earth he occupies it for a specific reason — to create relationship for other things. That is the mechanical side of life and even the masters have to appear to be mechanical in the form of mind and body — and yet they are not.

So we can say that for all your waking hours you have something to do — observe yourself. You don't have to worry about putting off anything to do it; you don't have to worry about setting aside time. The experiment which is life, your life, is going on continually. You are the scientist; life is the experiment; and your mind and your body are the reaction.

The scientist, when he goes into his laboratory, doesn't

judge during the experiment. Neither must you. Because, as I said, it will be the mind judging the mind. Even though you see yourself getting angry you are not allowed to say 'That is wrong'. If you see yourself ignoring the dear old lady who has just fallen down in the street, you must not say 'Aren't I terrible', and rush across to help her.

You are the scientist observing your reaction. You cannot observe if you are judging. We are trying to see ourselves as we are. Man does not see life as it is. If he saw it as it is he would see it as a harmony. He would see there is no good or bad; there is just harmony, and all things are right.

If you do anything that is false and you have the fortitude to continue to watch yourself it will stop, and what will be left will be you. It takes fortitude and courage but there is no doubt you will change.

The more you pursue this way of living the more your old friends will abandon you because your personality will change. This is because most personality is false — because it is trying. There is an essential personality in man that has to be reached by manhood, by tremendous work on yourself, by understanding, by separation from mind. There is no other way.

We will now consider the other half of this method — meditation. The instructions I give you are not essential. They are only aids. This whole teaching is an aid — if you don't need it, don't do it. But if you are not free then you need it.

In the beginning we are using mind. Mind has to have a path. Mind always moves in straight lines. Its morality is a straight line, so is its justice. We use the straight line as a method to trick mind into going towards its own doom — stillness — so that you never worry again, never become anguished, and know wisdom.

You will have noticed that I seldom answer questions in terms of yes and no. I skirt around the question and concentrate on the issues it raises because my object is to reach your understanding. The understanding is within you but it is fragmented. You need someone to pull it together and when it is pulled together you find you have a greater mass. This teaching pulls you together, makes you understand that the things you have been seeing for years have a direction and are not just accident.

I want you to understand the reason for meditation. Everybody meditates already; you meditate to learn anything. If you are an architect, in the beginning, you have to learn through the mind. Learning means that you have devoted time and effort to sitting and attending on a certain subject. As a result, or to the degree that you have devoted your time and effort to that subject, you absorb knowledge, but you also create another product. That is the understanding of your subject, and one of the vital ingredients of this is love. Love in the form of interest. If you love a subject it is much easier to do, for the movement of love whether outside or within is always towards union. You never have any difficulty with a subject you love or a person you love. So if you love the subject greatly you find that you give more time and effort — although it is not an effort to do what you love — and you gather more knowledge and out comes understanding.

You do not think when you love your job, except as a secondary supplementary action to your understanding. Your understanding is what takes the mediocrity out of you. Anyone who has just a knowledge of the job, and that means most people, is just ordinary and mediocre in it. But the person who loves it is the one who understands it, the brilliant one. There is another thing that gives brilliance but I am not dealing with that aspect of it tonight.

Understanding is the brilliance or genius in any job because understanding is higher than thought. It is the thing we are after. The thing which in architecture learns to add up, measure a wall and so on, is mind. And you may have noticed in your failings as I have in mine, that when I have to use knowledge or mind without the supporting genius of understanding, I am mediocre and I am never happy with the job. But if I am able to use my understanding I feel creative and delighted, and I feel in a sort of heaven, because consciousness is heaven.

You will notice that architecture is a subject outside yourself. When you meditate on yourself you meditate on something that is not outside yourself. It is the same in the beginning with meditation as architecture: you start to get knowledge for mind, and to the degree that you study, you break through the knowledge barrier and reach understanding.

It takes six years before a student doctor, working five or six days a week, twelve hours a day, is considered reasonably competent. I don't promise you any shorter period to know yourself, but the beauty of it is that you have been doing it unconsciously all your lives, so you have a start on the doctor. But remember even after six years he is still inexperienced. Here the analogy ends. It is not a quick job yet there is a journey's end, where you become the leader of your field. And to be the leader in this field is to be the leader of yourself.

To study ourselves we have to begin with ourselves. If I ask you what you are I will receive many descriptions because it is impossible for you to say what you are yet. In learning something outside yourself you accumulate knowledge. In gaining self-knowledge you do the reverse — you shed knowledge or the impressions you have of what you are.

You already regard yourself as a complete personality, otherwise you could not perform in the world as you do. You have aspirations or desires but you pursue them as this same amazingly complete identity you call you.

There are many subjects like architecture you do not know. Everyone is incomplete in this 'outside' way and no-one minds admitting it. But as yourself you feel you are complete.

Are you complete? At this moment you would be the first to admit you are not. Yet if someone outside suggests you are lacking in some way you feel hurt or insulted. Man takes offence so easily because he likes to believe he has all the admirable qualities, not having them questioned in him. He will sometimes admit his shortcomings in a friendly atmosphere but as soon as he is deliberately accused he will defend, resent and oppose or justify. Obviously he is a mixture of what he is and what he imagines he is. That is our problem. Self-knowledge is the discarding of what we imagine ourselves to be — the false in us. And when we rid ourselves of the false what remains will clearly be what is true or what we really are.

Where are we to begin if we don't know who we are? With one thing we are certain — the body. We observe the body with the mind. The unmastered mind cannot remain still. It has to have something to concentrate on or it will wander, so we give it the body. We do not give it a statue of the Buddha to meditate on as some people advise, because if we lose the statue we might not be able to meditate. Wherever we are we can begin with our body.

The directions I am going to give you are guides, and only guides.

It is customary to meditate in the sitting position, but some people have to lie down. Whatever you find works is right for you.

You should meditate morning and night. In the beginning you need quiet because noise will distract you. The mind is the enemy and it wants to run in every direction so it is not an easy job to make it attend where you want it to. You should meditate for up to ten minutes. There is no point in sitting when the mind gets restless.

You want a room with minimum lighting. Use any chair as long as you sit upright. Man is so unused to observing himself in this position that as soon as he sits and goes quiet he takes it as a command to go to sleep.

Have your feet together on the ground, knees comfortably apart, hands on your lap or lightly clasped. The back should be straight. If you slump you will tend to go to sleep. Look straight ahead with your eyes closed. Take three or four deep breaths.

Now put your attention on the body. There is movement and sensation in every part of it. Look at the fingers; you will have distinct feeling there. Look at your lips, your toes. Feel what's happening at the back of your neck and head — you may feel your heartbeat there.

Experience the joints which have a sensation of their own, the gums, the teeth. Go all around your body and you will discover sensations you never knew existed. You are now beginning to discover something new about yourself.

Meditation is not concentration. Meditation is not meditation on anything at all. It begins with observation of your own inner state of body and mind and is achieved in silence. Later you can use it as a process of investigation and discovery of truth and fact, but that comes after the mind is stilled.

The object of meditation is to become the master of your mind so that it lies still, open and resilient, waiting for your commands. You can only achieve this state by bringing the attention of the mind onto yourself and gradually drawing back from it. When you experience the stillness — even a brief respite from the restless movement of the ever-thinking mind — you will know a new freedom.

What is the difference between sleep and this stillness?

Sleep is completely mechanical. Our object is to become conscious, so if we go to sleep without our acquiescence then we are going into unconsciousness.

One object of meditation is to know the body asleep — to see your body asleep, breathing beautifully, while you are awake. Meditation is the body asleep, the mind transparent, and the consciousness just being.

Don't be discouraged if you do go off to sleep, there is no such thing as failure as long as you are making the effort. Don't strive too hard though, relax.

This is a way of poise and relaxation, not concentrated effort, except when you are overcoming and battling with yourself which is another stage of self-knowledge. The time does come when affliction hits all men and women but they seldom use their affliction to advantage. Affliction, worry and trouble are there for man to use to gain consciousness. But man regards affliction as something to be avoided, dodged, and if he is the cause of trouble, to escape by making excuses. Later on may come dreadful months of affliction and suffering but when it is all over you say 'I would have it all a hundred times worse for what I have gained'.

I have realised in the last couple of days that what I have been thinking about morality was not actually morality at all.

You have to watch morality because it is a mind-made thing. In some countries you can have three wives and in England you cannot. Morality varies from society to society, therefore you cannot talk of it in terms of truth.

The truth is that there is justice, but the justice of life is not the justice of man because man's justice always deals with objects outside himself. Man's justice allows him to go to war and kill, but not to kill at other times. This is a limping, halting justice but it is the best that mind can come up with.

113

The justice that we deal with is the justice of the totality of life — that all things to be are necessary and all things necessary are good, if only you can become a part of it, consciously.

In that existence is justice, and that justice includes man's justice, will and knowledge. It includes everything, but it is not a compromise and it does not vary. Man thinks that death is wrong otherwise he would not mourn when someone dies. He wouldn't think it terrible when men are killed in an air-crash or on the roads. Why is it terrible? Does man really think it is? Of course he doesn't, but he lies to himself and society that he cares. He lives a lie. But what we want is the fact of life not what man pretends to be sorry for, and then perpetuates.

Sorrow is the other side of beauty but sadness always has an object. Sadness is of mind and is a corrupt state; sorrow is not.

What is the difference between concern and worry?

People say 'Wouldn't you be worried if your child was dying?' I would reply 'No, concerned but certainly not worried'.

Worry is a state of split-personality, a state of ignorance. Men will say to you that everybody worries, but this is not so. I know one person anyway who doesn't. If your child is dying, and you are concerned, that means you are related to an object in life by the movement of life itself. This concern gives rise to emotion. Emotion is a conflict that man cannot escape while he occupies a body and a mind. Emotion is the product of conflict and conflict is the desire to change what is. The child is sick. I want to change the fact and make him better. Emotion in man very quickly leads to worry. There is no reason for man to worry, but to understand this he has to become the master of his mind because it is the mind that worries.

If I worry I will not be efficient and my child, who is very sick, will die. If I am concerned, I will act quickly because this conflict make's my whole being act quickly. I will say unconsciously 'My object is to save this child. How, using my intellect, can I do it?' I then say, 'I have to get him to a doctor'. I must find the doctor's address, get the car. You will notice there is no worry here; there is only action, awareness, although there is concern. Concern has an object. It is a beautiful state and in it you are efficient. You go from fact to fact — pick up the child, put it in the car, get a rug. You are efficient. You look at the facts that are required using the wonderful faculty of reason. You get the child to the doctor and the crisis is out of your hands. Then, if you are the master of your mind and yourself, you cut off.

But before cutting off you ask yourself if you have done your duty, whether there is anything you could still do. You look inside for the answer. You can't ask anyone because we are now in self-knowledge, working efficiently. You say 'I am not the doctor. If I were to break in there I could do nothing. I have done everything I can. I will go to sleep and arrange for someone to call me'.

Now let us have a look at worry. Worry never has an object. You can think it has but it does not. It does not operate in awareness. Worry deals in imagination and it doesn't have an object because it goes round in circles. To have an object you have to have an aim, to go towards something. Worry goes from impression to impression, not from fact to fact. The impression is 'my child might die' and as soon as you use the word 'might' in that context you are using impressions. So whenever you want to stop worry use it for self-observation.

Every time you begin to worry observe what worry is, see

115

its stupidity, your own insanity. You are a man who is supposed to be master of himself, supposed to have free-will. Who would give free-will to a person who worries?

Mind has to be stilled by observation, by going in and in day after day, by the processes that I have described. Mind cannot be defeated by opposition. Mind's momentum is opposition, and that is why you must never judge what mind does in yourself.

Truth is all there; there is nothing to be added to it, nothing to be taken away. It is there forever, and if you discover a truth now and two years later bring your attention onto it again, you will find it still there exactly the same because truth never changes.

I rely on that. When I speak it is this integrity of life that allows me my authority because whenever I look I see it. That is why I never have to argue, never have to be afraid of contradiction. But of course contradiction will appear and if ever you hear it there is a reason and your duty is to ask about it.

You have to discover that in a strange way truth is contradiction, and yet at the same time maintains the whole. This is beauty, but mind cannot understand it. Mind says the opposite to yes is no, and that's the end of it. Then truth 'laughs' and says 'I'll show you later, when you can understand it!' — You would be surprised how often I listen to myself, because consciousness speaks through me and my mind listens and there is I the listener and I the speaker.

Truth is discovered, not remembered; knowledge is remembered. Truth is discovered from moment to moment. As long as the mind is still, consciousness looks wherever it wants to and sees the truth, as real as rocks on the beach.

Information about other books, tapes, videos and seminars by Barry Long can be obtained via:

The Barry Long Foundation,
BCM Box 876, London WC1N 3XX, England.

The Barry Long Centre,
Box 5277, Gold Coast MC, Queensland 4217, Australia.